Bloom's

GUIDES

Nathaniel Hawthorne's
The Scarlet Letter

CURRENTLY AVAILABLE

1984
All the Pretty Horses
Beloved
Brave New World
Cry, The Beloved Country
Death of a Salesman
Hamlet
The Handmaid's Tale
The House on Mango Street
I Know Why the Caged Bird Sings
The Scarlet Letter
To Kill a Mockingbird

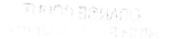

Bloom's
GUIDES

Nathaniel Hawthorne's
The Scarlet Letter

Edited & with an Introduction
by Harold Bloom

CHELSEA HOUSE
PUBLISHERS
A Haights Cross Communications Company
Philadelphia

A Haights Cross Communications ⚡ Company

Printed and bound in the United States of America.

First Printing
1 3 5 7 9 8 6 4 2

Library of Congress Cataloging-in-Publication Data

Nathaniel Hawthorne's The scarlet letter / edited and with an introduction by Harold Bloom.
     p. cm. — (Bloom's guides)
Includes bibliographical references and index.
  ISBN 0-7910-7563-X (hardcover) — ISBN 0-7910-7767-5 (pbk.) 1. Hawthorne, Nathaniel, 1804-1864. Scarlet letter. 2. Mothers and daughters in literature. 3. Massachusetts—In literature. 4. Puritans in literature. 5. Adultery in literature. 6. Women in literature. I. Title: Scarlet letter. II. Bloom, Harold. III. Series.
  PS1868.N38 2003
  813'.3—dc22
                                          2003016892

Chelsea House Publishers
1974 Sproul Road, Suite 400
Broomall, PA 19008-0914

www.chelseahouse.com

Contributing editor: Michael Terry Cisco
Cover design by Takeshi Takahashi
Layout by EJB Publishing Services

Contents

Introduction

Harold Bloom

The Western authorities on a nearly universal malady, sexual jealousy, are Shakespeare, Hawthorne, Freud, and Proust. *The Scarlet Letter*, one of the double handful of great American novels, is in some of its aspects untouched by the madness of jealousy, despite its pervasive theme of adultery. Only when Roger Chillingworth is the focus does Hawthorne's prose-romance take on the dissonances that recall Shakespeare's *Othello* and *The Winter's Tale*, and that prophesy Freud's and Proust's analyses of jealous obsessiveness. Chillingworth is both a devil and an avenging angel, at once sadist and masochist, not only ambiguous in his own nature but extraordinarily ambivalent toward the Reverend Mr. Dimmesdale, his timid and equivocal usurper. Dimmesdale and Chillingworth are one another's victims, and yet each needs the other in order to go on living. The reader is likely to note that Chillingworth frequently seems more a portrait of Satan than of a seventeenth-century scholar-physician. In some ways the cuckolded husband of Hester Prynne is as occult a figure as Pearl—the faery-child of Hester and Dimmesdale—or Mistress Hibbins the witch. Much of what we think of as human psychology seems as irrelevant to Chillingworth as it does to Pearl and Mistress Hibbins. And yet the psychology of sexual jealousy is very relevant to Chillingworth: it helps illuminate the strangeness of his conduct, toward Dimmesdale in particular. The Shakespearean version of sexual jealousy—essentially inherited by all subsequent authors—is transmuted by Milton's Satan before it reaches Chillingworth. Something of the aura of Satan playing Peeping Tom as he spies upon Adam and Eve still lingers as Chillingworth contemplates Hester and Dimmesdale. But the archetype remains Shakespeare's Iago, conniving the destruction of Othello and Desdemona in order to enhance his own sense of self, or what Milton's Satan called his "sense of injured merit."

Sexual jealousy as a sense of injured merit may, in the last analysis, be the fear that there will not be enough space or enough time for oneself. In Chillingworth's instance, the extended interval that he seeks might be interpreted as the sadist's desire to prolong his satisfaction at his victim's torments, yet that would be inadequate to the complexity of Hawthorne's art. When Chillingworth desperately attempts to prevent Dimmesdale from pronouncing his revelation of guilt, we hear a multitude of motives mingling together:

> "Madman, hold! What is your purpose?" whispered he. "Wave back that woman! Cast off this child! All shall be well! Do not blacken your fame, and perish in dishonor! I can yet save you! Would you bring infamy on your sacred profession?"

We may doubt Chillingworth's concern for the good name of the clergy, but he certainly does have a considerable psychic investment both in the survival and in the reputation of Dimmesdale. For artistic reasons that have to do with preserving the romance element in *The Scarlet Letter*, Hawthorne does not allow himself, or us, an acute psychological analysis of Chillingworth (or of Pearl or Mistress Hibbins). If you do the devil's work, then you become the devil, and so we have the oddity that Iago and Chillingworth become considerably more diabolic than Milton's Satan ever manages to become, despite his titanic efforts. Chillingworth quite forgets he is a man, and becomes an incarnate jealousy instead. His pride in keeping Dimmesdale alive is augmented by the clergyman's public image of holiness, while Chillingworth's deepest pleasure resides in the conviction that Dimmesdale ultimately will share in the physician's spiritual damnation, linked for eternity by their roles in Hester's tragic story.

Dimmesdale, caught between Hester and Chillingworth, has neither the blessed strength of Hester's balked capacity for life nor the infernal strength of Chillingworth's impotent hatred for life. The minister's character and personality, despite his acute sensibility, render him too weak to be tragic. When we think of *The Scarlet Letter* as a portrait of human character in dramatic conflict with itself, we are compelled to center upon Hester, whose power of endurance is almost frightening in its sustained intensity. Dimmesdale is so pallid in comparison that we wonder how he ever provoked an extraordinary passion in Hester, who is so much superior to him in her capacity for an authentic life. Subtle as Hawthorne is throughout the novel, he is pragmatically sinuous in finding a multitude of ways to persuade us of Hester's sexual power. When he speculates that, but for Pearl, Hester would have been a second Ann Hutchinson, a major religious rebel against seventeenth-century American Puritanism, he associates his heroine with a violent energy, "the flesh and blood of action," that can only be sexual. Then *The Scarlet Letter* would have been a realistic tragedy, since Hester in full rebellion would have become a prefeminist martyr, immolated by the righteous men of Puritan Boston.

Readers now, as we have just passed the Millenium, may be tempted to undervalue the courage and physical stamina that Hester manifests in maintaining her seven-year defiance of her entire society: its religion, morality, and sense of election by God and by divinely decreed history. Hawthorne never violates her dignity, her self-reliance, her loyalty to the unworthy Dimmesdale. At least a century ahead of her own time, Hester would be fierce enough to die for her sense of self were it not, as we have seen, for her maternal obligations. Yet she is too large and passionate a being to have any sense of injured merit; within limits she bears her outcast status as the cost of her confirmation as a natural woman, and her consciousness of her own "sin" is highly ambivalent. It is difficult not to feel that Hester Prynne is as much Nathaniel Hawthorne as Emma Bovary is Gustave Flaubert. Hester indeed is a Hawthorne-like artist; her embroidery is a metaphor for her creator's narrative art, and the scarlet letter she wears is defiantly an aesthetic artifact, representing art far more truly than it represents adultery, though hardly in the view of Puritan Boston.

Hawthorne's implicit celebration of Hester's sexual nature is also necessarily a celebration of her highly individual will, which is more a post-Emersonial nineteenth-century version of the Protestant will than it is a Puritan kind of seeing, saying, and acting. A Puritan will could not survive isolation; Hester's will belongs to a different order of American spiritual consciousness, one that can find freedom in solitude, even when that solitude is a punishment imposed by a repressive society. Hawthorne informs us that the scarlet letter has "the effect of a spell, taking her out of the ordinary relations with humanity, and enclosing her in a sphere by herself." Since the Puritan public sphere is marked by sadism, hypocrisy, and (as portrayed by Hawthorne with particular skill) a shocking lack of compassion, we can wonder why Hester does not take Pearl and depart into what might be a wholesome exile. The answer, as Hawthorne intimates, is deeply pathetic: having chosen Dimmesdale, Hester refuses to abandon what she regards as her true marriage. When he dies, his head supported by her bosom, he is still totally unworthy of her, and yet she has remained true to the integrity of her own will.

Biographical Sketch

Nathaniel Hawthorne was born July 4, 1804, the son of Elizabeth Manning Hathorne and Nathaniel Hathorne, Sr., who was descended from an interrogator at the Salem witch trials. (Hawthorne added the "w" to his name around 1830). In 1809, after the death of his father, Hawthorne, his mother, and his two sisters lived at the home of his maternal grandparents. His early studies took place at Samuel Archer's School. In his childhood, Hawthorne read extensively in classic literature, absorbing Edmund Spenser's *The Faery Queene*, John Bunyon's *Pilgrim's Progress*, Shakespeare, Sir Walter Scott, and endless gothic romances. The sentiments of these works saturate his writing, lending them a sense of self-knowledge and precision and, at their greatest heights, great insight into human character.

This grounding in literature stood Hawthorne in good stead during his college years at Bowdoin College in Maine, where he joined the Athenean Literary Society and began to write the first of many short stories. His classmates included poet Henry Wadsworth Longfellow and Franklin Pierce, the future president of the United States, who became one of Hawthorne's closest friends. Although he was a mediocre student who could not be bothered to study any topics that did not catch his eye, the years at Bowdoin had an enormous influence on Hawthorne's career.

From Bowdoin, Hawthorne returned to Salem, to the "chamber under the eaves" at his mother's house where he was to spend many solitary years. From 1825 to 1837 Hawthorne perfected his craft, writing tales, sketches, and ideas for novels and poems. During this time he developed the moral universe that would undergird his later works, reading extensively in both classic and contemporary literature and jotting his responses in his voluminous notebooks. He self-published his first novel, *Fanshawe*, based on his Bowdoin years, but embarrassed at his early effort withdrew the book and destroyed every copy he could find. Two years after the publication of *Fanshawe*, in 1830, Hawthorne published his first short story, "The Hollow of the Three Hills," in the Salem *Gazette*. Over the next few years he published several sketches, semi-autobiographical works and tales in various magazines, but did not receive any critical or popular attention until he published his first collection of short stories, *Twice-Told Tales*, in 1837; an expanded edition appeared in 1842.

In 1837, Hawthorne, who was famously taciturn, self-contained and cool in temperament, fell deeply in love. Sophia Peabody was also from Salem, an invalid whose cheerfulness and good temper were unaffected by her illness. She and Hawthorne became secretly engaged, partially because they feared the disapproval of her family, and partially because they enjoyed the delicious spark of their hidden relationship. Hawthorne realized that when he was married his meager earnings as a writer would not be enough to support Sophie, and began lobbying for a political appointment. Since his time at Bowdoin, he had been an ardent supporter of the Democratic party in which his friend Franklin Pierce was active. Through his connections in government, Hawthorne became the official Measurer of Coal and Salt at the Boston Custom House. Although the post paid well, Hawthorne found that the long hours and physical demands kept him from his writing, and after two years he realized that he had to find another way of supporting himself.

Influenced by Sophia's interest in the Transcendentalist movement, Hawthorne invested money in an experimental Utopian community, Brook Farm, and spent a year there before the romance of farming palled. After leaving Brook Farm, Hawthorne devoted himself once again to writing full-time in the attic of his family's house. In 1842 he and Sophia were finally married, and moved to the Old Manse in Concord, Massachusetts. Their three years there were the happiest time of Hawthorne's life, as he wrote, spent time with Henry David Thoreau, Margaret Fuller and other writers, and worked in the garden with Sophia. While at the Old Manse, Sophia gave birth to their first child, Una, in 1844; a delicate child, her health was a constant concern to her parents. Una was followed by a brother, Julian, in 1846 and a sister, Rose, in 1851.

Between 1842 and 1846, when he published his second collection of tales, *Mosses from an Old Manse*, Hawthorne worked steadily and published many of his stories in magazines. After a frustrating stint as Surveyor of the Salem Custom House, which he describes humorously in the introduction to *The Scarlet Letter*, Hawthorne embarked on the most prolific and successful part of his career.

The Scarlet Letter, Hawthorne's tragic, brilliant tale of passion and retribution, possesses a strength and depth that he was never to achieve in any of his other works. The novel attained immediate public success, both financially and critically, upon its publication in 1850. The overwhelming acclaim invigorated Hawthorne and spurred an astonishing amount of work. In the next two years he wrote *The House of the Seven Gables* (1851), *The Blithedale Romance* (1852), and a campaign biography of his friend Franklin Pierce, as well as a collection of tales and two children's books. Even this prodigious output was not enough to support the family, though, and in 1853 he accepted the position of United States Consul to England from President Franklin Pierce.

The years in England solved Hawthorne's financial problems and introduced him to the glorious art and culture of Europe, but dealt a fatal blow to his artistic powers. From 1853 until his death in 1864, he published only one novel, *The Marble Faun* (1860), and a collection of articles and essays, *Our Old Home* (1863). After his post in England, the Hawthornes lived in Rome and Florence from 1857 to 1859, and returned to Concorde in 1860, living at his mother's home, The Wayside, until the author's death. Hawthorne was frequently ill, and deeply distressed by the looming Civil War that threatened to tear the country apart. Despite the presence of his family, Hawthorne had begun to feel an acute sense of loneliness and loss, an inability to communicate deeply either personally or in his writing. He began work again and again on novels, only to break off in frustration. By March of 1864 Sophia was frightened by his haggard, weak appearance, by the light that had gone out of his eyes. On May 18, 1864, while on a journey to Plymouth, New

Hampshire with Franklin Pierce, Hawthorne died in his sleep, leaving a legacy of imagination and perception unmatched in American fiction.

The Story Behind the Story

"There is evil in every human heart," wrote Nathaniel Hawthorne in his notebooks. In Hawthorne's greatest works, his somber, mysterious, carefully structured prose analyzes the problem of sin inherent in the beautiful and terrible world humans have created; *The Scarlet Letter* is his masterpiece on sin, terrible secrecy, and retribution.

Nathaniel Hathorne was born on the fourth of July, 1804, in Salem, Massachusetts to a family that had resided in Salem for well over a hundred years. Among the men who interrogated those persons brought before the witch court of 1692, the records include a Judge John Hathorne. Nathaniel Hawthorne chose to write historical fictions, "romances" or semi-fantastic stories, drawing on New England's past, and this also placed him in a strange relationship to these ancestors; he was connected to them in the material, and yet detached from them artistically. That he himself would have been criticized harshly by his Puritan forbears for wasting his life writing frivolous stories was not something he doubted. A passage from his notebooks is revealing:

'What is he?' murmurs one gray shadow of my forefathers to the other. 'A writer of story-books! What kind of business in life,—what mode of glorifying God, or being serviceable to mankind in his day and generation,—may that be? Why, the degenerate fellow might as well have been a fiddler!'

In 1846, Hawthorne's friends in the Democratic party, including future president and Hawthorne's old college friend from Bowdoin, Franklin Pierce, nominated him for a surveyor's job at the Custom House in Salem. He had tried and failed to maintain the family with his pen, writing both serious literature and less inspired, less personal commercial work. His second child, Julian, had just been born, and the family badly needed an income. Unfortunately, Hawthorne acquired his post in a rather heated competition, and his success earned him a number of enemies in the local administration. What is worse, he detested the work; while it was not an especially demanding position, Hawthorne felt his post was sapping his creative powers, and neutering his soul. For the first eighteen months of his employment at the Custom House, Hawthorne does not appear to have written anything. Eventually he resumed writing short stories again, but progress was slow. Late in 1848, finding short story writing no longer appealed to him, Hawthorne cautiously decided once again to turn his hand to novel-writing, which he had not attempted since his failed first novel, *Fanshawe*, twenty years earlier.

As it happened, he would have ample freedom to work on his new project: when the Whigs replaced the Democrats in Washington, early in 1849, Hawthorne lost his post; critics speculate that the heated political arena he found himself in contributed to his acrimonious tone in *The Scarlet Letter*. Hawthorne lost more than his job in 1849—he also lost his mother. He had been a dutiful son, and her death was an especially heavy blow to him. Hawthorne did not remove himself from Salem right away, but, by the end of the year, he relocated his family to Lenox, Massachusetts. It was during this time, between his departure from the Custom House and his departure from Salem, that *The Scarlet Letter* was composed.

The novel was a surprising literary and commercial success when in first appeared in 1850, selling out its first run in just ten days. Even halfway into the nineteenth century, American literary markets were dominated by English imports, and American writers were still struggling to establish a distinctly American literary idiom. The New York-based group of writers and editors known as Young America began to promote Hawthorne's work as an example of a new and distinctly American literary style. It was largely through their attentions that Hawthorne was introduced to Herman Melville, who wrote a violently affirmative review of *Mosses from an Old Manse* for the *Literary World*, comparing Hawthorne favorably to Shakespeare. This review, along with the popularity of *The Scarlet Letter*, helped to solidify Hawthorne's reputation as an important American writer, as one of the first members of an American canon.

Henry James, one of the most important writers of the generation succeeding Hawthorne's, wrote the first substantial treatise on his work. "*The Scarlet Letter*," he writes, "contains little enough of gaiety or hopefulness. It is densely dark, with a single spot of vivid colour in it; and it will probably long remain the most consistently gloomy of English novels of the first order. But I just now called it the author's masterpiece, and I imagine it will continue to be, for other generations than ours, his most substantial title to fame." History proved James right, as *The Scarlet Letter* has become one of the most commonly-read and best-known nineteenth-century American novels.

List of Characters

Hester Prynne

Born in England to a decayed noble family, Hester was consigned to a loveless marriage of convenience with Master Prynne, later known as Roger Chillingworth. After a brief season in Amsterdam, it was decided that they would join the Puritans in Boston; Hester ventured across the Atlantic first, her husband planning to join her later. After roughly a year, during which time she had received no word of her husband, and many speculated he had died en route to America, Hester committed adultery with the local minister, Arthur Dimmesdale. She became pregnant, and so the crime was discovered and punished. A stately, robust, and darkly beautiful woman, she seems to retain some of the grace and poise of the aristocracy from which she is descended; and she perhaps resembles her ancestors in her self-reliance and confidence in her own conscience. Hester exhibits immense strength of character during the course of the novel's events, accepting her punishment without resentment, and yet without resigning her authority over herself, even over her own sin. She becomes a benefactor to the community that has judged her sternly and ostracized her for a not incomprehensible crime; she becomes a sign and a prophet, as well, to the Puritan community of Boston, accumulating different interpretations as time goes by. Hester is severely tested, not so much by the gross cruelty of her community towards her, but by her concern over the fate of Pearl, her daughter. Her noble resolve not to expose Dimmesdale nevertheless places Pearl in moral jeopardy. By the end of the novel, she is desperate enough to agree to run away to Europe with Dimmesdale and live with him in sin.

Roger Chillingworth

Hester Prynne's husband, the slightly deformed Master Prynne, had dedicated his youth to study, only to find middle age lonelier and less habitable than he had expected. Longing for a family, his eye settled on young Hester, and they were married. Having sent Hester ahead of him to America, Prynne came shortly thereafter, only to be taken and held captive for a year by the natives. Upon emerging at last from the forest, he discovers his wife being held up to public opprobrium for adultery; to avoid humiliation, and to better facilitate his search for the father of his wife's illegitimate child, he adopts the name "Roger Chillingworth." While he is able to forgive Hester, who promises to protect the secret of his identity as closely as she does that of her lover, he cannot bring himself to forgive the man who has wronged them both. In time, having set himself up as a doctor in Boston, he artfully discovers the true culprit, and sets himself the task of hounding and exacerbating Dimmesdale's bad conscience into morbid and ultimately life-threatening personal torture. He perverts the purposes of medicine, seeking to prolong life only to prolong suffering. By adopting the role of Dimmesdale's self-appointed tormentor, Chillingworth unwittingly sets in motion his own decomposition. As the novel draws to a close, he is only the withered husk of the nobler man he had formerly been.

Arthur Dimmesdale
The minister for the town of Boston, Arthur Dimmesdale was educated in England, and brought with him to America a great power of persuasive speech, extensive learning, and a simple, almost angelic faith. Where Chillingworth possesses an invasive, penetrating eye, Dimmesdale has a soft yet penetrating voice; he does not hector and terrify his congregation in the course of his sermons, but persuades and inspires them by speaking directly to their souls. Dimmesdale is handsome, however, and, drawn no doubt as much by her inner nobility as by her outward beauty, he commits adultery with Hester Prynne, who bears his child. He does not confess his crime to the community he serves in order to continue his good work, and, in fact, his secret sin makes him an even more effective minister; unlike all the other Puritan authorities, he is unable to sit in complacent judgment of others. Instead of facing public condemnation, Dimmesdale punishes himself in private, subjecting himself to torments—made worse by

Chillingworth—that are ultimately far more damaging than the official punishment would have been. He is not exactly a hypocrite, since, in the first place, the Puritan religion regards all men to be sinners unworthy of salvation, and, in the second place, he does not deceive himself into believing in his innocence, standing in stark contrast to such characters as Governor Bellingham, who is callous and unforgiving in the name of Christianity. He saves Hester from the damning temptation to hate and do evil to the community by preventing the Boston authorities from taking Pearl away from her. Finally, as he feels his life ebbing away, Dimmesdale makes his confession, and saves Pearl as well.

Pearl Prynne

Pearl is the only major character in the novel to be born in America. She is also the character most fundamentally at stake in the novel; born in prison and several months old before ever seeing broad daylight, she is an otherworldly, fairy or imp-like child, a fatherless changeling and seemingly not fully human. A graceful girl of uncannily perfect beauty, but with an unruly, mercurial personality, she has the potential to become truly monstrous, or else an astoundingly worthy human being. Formed in the womb during a period in Hester's life of profound interior warfare, Pearl came into the world with these elements of strife mixed up in her: she is their embodiment. While not a cold or unloving child, she cannot fail to feel and resent her mother's refusal to tell her who her father is, and, in her own way, she stubbornly insists upon the normalization of her relationship to the world. In fact, Pearl cannot be fooled; she instinctively perceives Chillingworth's demonical malice, and seems to understand that Dimmesdale is her father, even if she cannot understand why no one will say that he is. When he finally acknowledges her before all of Boston, the spell that kept her from being entirely human is broken, and she is able to weep for him, to exhibit the empathy formerly absent in her.

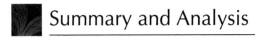

Summary and Analysis

The Scarlet Letter opens with an extended, trickily semi-autobiographical preface, which serves the book less as an overture than as a bridge linking the past, and this story, to the present, and perhaps to the modern art of self-referential fiction as well. *The Scarlet Letter* is not a record of historical fact, but it draws upon history; the scarlet letter that Hester Prynne wears is embroidered with gold thread, and likewise the historical information that Hawthorne draws upon to write his novel is embroidered with fictional events—these events, however, do not simply exploit history for background material—rather, they test our understanding of that past history, and attempt to resurrect from dry facts a living picture of the past, replete with all its moral complexity. History which does not take the complexity and ambiguity of past eras into account is nothing more than a series of morally reductive summary judgments on past events. The study of history teaches us that each generation judges the one preceding it according to the standards of its own time and place, and not according to the standards of that previous time. This judgment, therefore, is an anachronism—it is unjust. So, Hawthorne advocates a subtler, more sophisticated approach; he tries to revive the past and bring it before the present as though it were still able to answer the present's allegations with its own voice. He tries to show that the circumstances and conditions of past times were different. Most important of all, he tries to show that a reductive moral judgment about the past tells us nothing new, it merely reaffirms in the present what we already know.

So, just as Hawthorne has embroidered history to give us the scarlet letter, he also embroiders his own autobiography in this preface. Hawthorne took a job at Salem's Custom House in 1846. The Custom House, he suggests, is run in the same thoughtless, convention-bound way that prevailed in Puritan Boston. Indeed, some of the employees are almost old enough to remember Puritan Boston! Hawthorne invents a predecessor, Jonathan Pue, who is supposed to have written an imaginary record of the events in Hester Prynne's case. He even describes finding the scarlet letter itself, lying among Pue's documents. So, the account of the origin of the novel is also fictional. History is a collection of stories human beings tell about themselves each other and to those who will come after them; facts are involved in these stories, but they have a personal and philosophical significance which far outweighs the importance of these facts. It is a significance that emerges when one reads history critically, but without rushing to judgment.

The Scarlet Letter is a novel about judgment, and about the relations that arise between publicly trumpeted or imposed values and private moral decision. It is important to make this point at once, because *The Scarlet Letter* is too often imprecisely read as a condemnation of Puritan hypocrisy and intolerance; these are matters of concern for Hawthorne, but they are not the principal focus of the narrative. The Puritans provide an excellent example of provincial bigotry and unself-conscious inconsistency between theory and practice; Hawthorne does depict them, for the most part, as ignorant rabble. However, their hypocrisy and prejudice are not entirely taken for granted; rather, they are tested by the events of the novel and permitted to unfold in a variety of opinion. Even the vulgar Boston Puritans are not perfectly uniform; a plurality of opinion on a number of subjects, and gradual changes in opinion, is apparent among them.

Hawthorne commonly deals with moral crises which have both a cut-and-dry aspect on the one hand and a considerably more vague aspect on the other. Hester Prynne is definitely guilty of adultery, and, while the crime is unfortunate, it is not abominable. Despite the many mitigating circumstances, it is never represented as less than a crime—in fact, when Hester and Dimmesdale are tempted to run away together, this is represented as a moment of serious moral jeopardy. However firmly established Hester's guilt may be, such that the cause of her guilt is established as fact and may not be tampered with, the effects of her guilt introduce many ambiguities. As a result of her crime and her punishment, she becomes a great asset to the community, greater than she might otherwise have been. Dimmesdale becomes a more effective minister as a result of his secret guilt; the essential flaw in Hester's marriage is brought plainly into view.

As is usual with Hawthorne's novels, the plot is straightforward, with a minimum of events, dealing in the main with the interaction of characters in a basically fixed, many-layered predicament. It is set in Boston at the time of the Puritans. Hester Prynne is a beautiful young woman of formerly aristocratic stock; a Puritan, born in England, she married a studious older man she neither loved nor pretended to love, for reasons that are largely implied (he was lonely; his eye fell on her; somehow the marriage was arranged). Like the Pilgrims who settled the Plymouth colony in 1620, she and her husband move to Holland for a time, and then make plans to resettle in America. Hester is sent ahead of her husband, who then fails to arrive or to send any word. As time passes, she begins to suspect some mischance has waylaid him, perhaps a shipwreck, and that he may be dead. After roughly a year, she commits adultery with Arthur Dimmesdale, the young minister of Boston; their crime is more of a mutual lapse than a matter of wickedness or defiance to society, or even of passion. Plainly, they would make an excellent marriage, if she were free.

Hester becomes pregnant, and her crime cannot long be concealed. She is imprisoned, where she gives birth to a baby girl, Pearl Prynne. Although she is pressured by town officials to reveal the identity of the child's father, she refuses to do so. Dimmesdale, while bitterly tormented by guilt and sympathy for Hester's suffering, holds his peace; were he to be exposed, he could no longer serve the community as its minister, something he is amply able to do. Unlike the other Puritan ministers of the time, Dimmesdale is not a stentorian dogmatist loudly condemning sin, but a more spiritual, more uplifting sermonizer. His work in Boston clearly demonstrates that he is a man of superior abilities, deep faith, and possessing a rare capacity for self-sacrifice. It is precisely this aspect of his character that makes him most susceptible to anguish for Hester's suffering and his own sin. It also enables him to marvel at Hester's extraordinary strength of character, and to appreciate in full her sacrifice for him.

All of this is by way of back story. The novel opens with "**The Prison Door**," a brief chapter of three paragraphs which sets the scene by means of an extended description of a single symbolic element. This is the reader's first encounter with Hawthorne's Puritan Boston; "a throng of bearded men, in sad-colored garments and gray" and waiting for the door to their small prison house to open. The prison door separates the prisoners from the free citizens, the jail from the town; observing this scene, it is not immediately clear on which side of the door the Puritans are grouped. Immediately at the outset, and with considerable elegance, Hawthorne has established a double standard, such that the judgment of the Puritans is never represented without a contrary viewpoint. No one in Hawthorne's fiction is free to judge another; in putting up a heavy prison door "studded with iron spikes" they have bound themselves as much as they have bound their prisoners.

Before proceeding to the story, Hawthorne draws the reader's attention to a rose bush, growing up among the worthless and ugly plants surrounding the prison. Perhaps it had grown there from time immemorial, but some would say "it had sprung up under the footsteps of the sainted Ann Hutchinson, as she entered the prison-door." Ann Hutchinson was an early *antinomian*; she was persecuted by the Boston Puritans in the first years of the Massachussetts Bay Company's existence for rejecting (to put it simply) their judgmental and austere moral theology. After spending time in jail, she was expelled from the colony, and eventually killed in a massacre by Native Americans in New Rochelle, New York. Hawthorne explains that this story transpires fifteen or twenty years after the founding of Boston, which places the date between 1645 and 1650. Ann Hutchinson has been gone for no less than twelve years.

The prison door opens and the second chapter, "**The Market-Place**," begins. To a casual observer, Hawthorne explains, the grim demeanor of these Puritans would suggest that the perpetrator of some drastic crime were about to appear; but, in fact, this grimness is commonplace, and Puritanical discipline is so severe that even minor infractions, or differences of opinion in religious matters, is a matter of deep moral gravity to them. Hester Prynne will meet with no sympathy for her crime, but, on the other hand, she will not be mocked for her shame. In passing, Hawthorne mentions Mistress Hibbins, widow of the magistrate, who is widely rumored to be a witch—we will encounter her again later. The women of Puritan Boston are of "a coarser fibre" than women in Hawthorne's own time; they are hard-working, large, blunt-talking, and robust, not especially lady-like. Their disapproval of Hester is especially strong; some of the women exhibit signs of being jealous of Hester, without realizing it themselves, and from these comes the most vehement judgment.

Hester's much-anticipated first appearance now takes place, and it is important to take careful note of the manner in which Hawthorne presents her. The beadle (a sort of policeman and warder in one) draws her forward toward the door with his hand on her shoulder. Just within the door, she puts his hand off, "by an action marked with natural dignity and force of character," and emerges from the jail on her own, "as if by her own free will." She is carrying Pearl, her daughter, who is seeing the light of day for the first time; she holds Pearl in such a way as to conceal the letter on her chest, the embroidered A, for "Adultress." Pearl and the letter will be associated closely throughout the novel, so it is not insignificant that she and the letter should both appear at the same time. Hester shifts her grasp on Pearl so as not to hide the letter, "with a burning blush, and yet a haughty smile, and a glance that would not be abashed." Being an expert seamstress, Hester has embroidered the letter and included "fantastic flourishes of gold thread." She has transformed the mark of her shame into a rich ornament. In all this there is a profound mixture of shame and defiance; Hester accepts the law, the charge, the punishment, but she refuses to be replaced by them. Her destiny will remain her own to determine, and she has not resigned her rights as a human being.

Hawthorne describes Hester's appearance; she is a beautiful

woman, if somewhat sturdier of build than was fashionable for women in his own time. She is "lady-like," and later in the chapter she remembers her childhood home in England, with its "half-obliterated shield of arms over the portal, in token of antique gentility." Hester is therefore the descendent of a once-noble line, and perhaps retains some of their native poise and dignity of bearing—and sense of self-worth.

Hester is led to the platform in the market-place and exposed to the crowd. She must stand there and allow them to stare at her, to impose a heavy sense of inward guilt upon her. Hawthorne explains that, while Hester has the strength to bear insult, this demeaning public display taxes her to the utmost limit of her emotional endurance. Her mind takes refuge in images of the past, and in the process the reader is introduced to the bare facts of her case: her marriage in England to an old scholarly man "with the left shoulder a trifle higher than the right," and their subsequent removal to "a Continental city" (Amsterdam).

In "**The Recognition**," a new figure is introduced into the scene. Emerging from the wilderness, accompanied by a native guide, comes a small man "with a furrowed visage" and one shoulder higher than the other. This is her husband, who has chosen an extremely awkward day on which to rejoin his wife. Hester and her husband recognize each other, and a silent drama is played out within them. Feigning only casual interest, Master Prynne asks a bystander about Hester as though she were a stranger, and discovers the circumstances of her shame. She is standing not only in the presence of the crowd, but in that of the very governor of the colony and its chief religious authorities as well, all of whom are highly deficient in sympathy. John Wilson, the most revered minister in the colony, exhorts Hester to reveal her lover's name, even placing his hand on Dimmesdale's shoulder as he does so. We learn that Dimmesdale has opposed any attempt to force Hester to answer before we are introduced to him properly.

Arthur Dimmesdale is everything the other Puritan authorities are not; he is young, sensitive, sympathetic, tenderly spiritual, and wholly lacking in cruel instincts. Where Wilson and Bellingham are like stern, unforgiving Old Testament prophets, Dimmesdale is like an angel, or a child. Wilson commands Dimmesdale to speak to Hester, and he issues his first speech of the novel; he urges her to answer, saying "Be not silent from any mistaken pity and tenderness for him; for, believe me, Hester, though he were to step down from a high place, and stand there beside thee, on thy pedestal of shame, yet better were it so, than to hide a guilty heart through life." Just as the words of the other Puritan leaders stir an impulse to judge and condemn in the crowd, so Dimmesdale's words bring "the listeners into one accord of sympathy."

Why does Hester preserve Dimmesdale's secret? In part, clearly, out of respect for his good works, but more so because, in asserting her own free will, she must assert the free will of all. She cannot confess on someone else's behalf, no matter how tempting the prospect; Dimmesdale must confess on his own. It is not Hester's decision to make, nor is it fair for Dimmesdale to impose it upon her. She refuses, at great personal cost, to answer. Not only does she lose all chance of removing the scarlet letter from her chest, but she throws away Pearl's only opportunity to know her true father. "... my child must seek a heavenly Father; she shall never know an earthly one!" After a fire-and-brimstone sermon from Wilson, Hester, who has lapsed into a kind of delirious hard-mindedness in the course of her ordeal, is returned to the prison.

The next chapter is "**The Interview**." Once out of the public eye, Hester lapses into a state of intense emotional distress, and, as a man of science, who but her husband is called to attend her. Introducing himself as "Roger Chillingworth," he asks to be left alone with Hester; with the jailer out of the way, they are free to drop the pretense of being strangers to each other. He provides a drug for Pearl, who has also become distraught; when Hester hesitates to administer it, her husband answers "What should ail me to harm this misbegotten and miserable babe?" The drug proves to be effective, and Chillingworth then concocts a potion for his wife; "Even if I imagine a scheme of vengeance, what could I do better for my object than to let thee live,—than to give thee medicines against all harm and peril of life,—so that this burning shame may still blaze upon thy bosom?" This is the equivocal key to Chillingworth's character; he is a doctor who heals and harms at once. His excellence in medicine is a sign of malice, or cold curiosity, and none of sympathy or compassion.

All the same, he does not ultimately blame or despise Hester for her crime. "It was my folly, and thy weakness ... from the moment when we came down the old church-steps together, a married pair, I might have beheld the bale-fire of that scarlet letter blazing at the end of our path!" Mismatched in age and inclination, he both deformed and otherworldly with excessive study, cold and aloof—the marriage could not possibly have been a success. Hester, though little inclined to defend herself, points out that she "felt no love, nor feigned any" for her husband. Chillingworth grants the point; he, like Faust, found himself old and alone after many decades of study, and thought to try, before it was too late, to foster a loving family around himself. He accepts his failure, and promises Hester he has no intention of trying to avenge himself upon her. Toward her lover, however, he has no such magnanimous feelings; he presses her to confess his name, but she will not. Chillingworth is unfazed; while he has been compelled to accept his failure as a husband, he still has complete confidence in his powers of observation, even of detection. He is certain he will find out the identity of Hester's lover, and find his own way to punish him. In the meantime, he is willing to bargain with Hester; if she will not tell him the name of her lover, she may at least bind herself to a similar promise with regard to Chillingworth's true identity. In this way, Hester's social isolation will be reinforced by multiple obligations to conceal the truth of two identities, and, in so doing, she will undermine the identity of her own daughter, Pearl.

With chapter five, **"Hester and Her Needle,"** the more outrageous test of her mettle being over, it is now time for the daily trials to begin. Hester is now free to leave the prison, but her everyday life is hardly to be preferred to confinement. The scarlet letter is a burden she will wear until her death, and in life, "giving up her individuality, she would become the general symbol at which the preacher and moralist might point, in which they might vivify and embody their images of woman's frailty and sinful passion." Of course, she might simply choose to leave New England; but Hawthorne explains that Hester feels so completely transformed by her ordeal that it is as if she were born anew into the world, and bound by her very sin to the environs of Boston. This is not all. Hester's motive for remaining, at least as she explains it to herself, is "half a truth, half a self-delusion." She believes that, by remaining, she has some hope of redeeming herself; but, without acknowledging it, she also remains because she cannot bear to part with Dimmesdale. He alone in the world can share her shame, can understand her suffering; and she regards herself to be "connected in a union" with him—to be, in fact, his true wife. Hawthorne had, in his own way, a sharp understanding of what psychologists would later term "the unconscious." His characters frequently act on motives that they do not correctly or clearly perceive; and Hawthorne has no qualms about pointing to and plainly stating these motives for the benefit of his audience.

Hester and Pearl take up residence in a modest, isolated home on the outskirts of town. While the land there is barren, and the prospects poor, Hester is blessed with exceptional skill in embroidery. It is she, the rejected outcast, who makes the fine lace which adorns the colony's officials at state occasions—and departed loved ones in their coffins—and, most ironically of all, her linen is in high demand among the citizenry's "legitimate" offspring. Even Governor Bellingham himself wears some of Hester's needle-work on his ruff. "But it is not recorded that, in a single instance, her skill was called in aid to embroider the white veil which was to cover the pure blushes of a bride. The exception indicated the ever relentless vigor with which society frowned upon her sin." In any event, Hester is able to earn a meager living.

While Hester herself wears only the plainest clothes, Pearl, as the years pass, is dressed with "a fantastic ingenuity." Hester has not only skill, but a highly original taste; her work is genuinely beautiful. Furthermore, even though she herself is not far from poverty, Hester gives money to the poor, even to those who are better off than she, and spends her time fashioning simple clothing for them. In short, Hester is determined to contribute to Boston society, whether the Puritans of Boston like it or not. This resolve is all the more remarkable in light of the fact that "Every gesture, every word, and even the silence of those with whom she came in contact, implied, and often expressed, that she was banished...." Worst of all, her experience of sin has made her more sympathetically sensitive to it, so that she seems able, almost magically, to detect bad conscience when confronted with it. Hester finds herself compelled to convince herself repeatedly that the people around her are not all sinners like herself, or perhaps worse.

The reader is meant to understand that time is passing, that Hawthorne is describing typical events as they are generally played out in the years following Hester's sentencing. Pearl is growing into a young girl, into a character in the novel, and we find out more about her in the chapter, "**Pearl.**" Hester regards Pearl with great misgivings. "She knew that her deed had been evil; she could have no faith, therefore, that its result would be for good." She observes Pearl's growth and development with concern, and finds her a disturbingly remote, unsympathetic girl. Not exactly cold, Pearl is capable of whimsical delight, and of truly violent rage; but there is no love in her. Physically, Pearl is perfect, and clearly will grow up to become a beautiful woman. She possesses grace and a mercurial personality, and is potentially wild and unruly. Rules and discipline are meaningless to her, yet she is not malicious. Hester is frightened by Pearl's strangeness; she finds her daughter unintelligible, an enigma. Time and again Hawthorne compares Pearl to a fairy child, a changeling, an imp, or witch-child. Pearl is not fully human, because she does not experience rooted human emotions; it's as though she lives in a dream. When Hester musingly asks her, "... whence didst thou come?" Pearl replies, "It is thou that must tell me!" While Pearl cannot entirely understand her situation, she already knows that her mother is hiding something from her.

As shall be made clear later on, roughly three years have passed altogether since the events which opened the novel. In "**The Governor's Hall**," Hester presents herself to Governor Bellingham, ostensibly to deliver to him a pair of gloves he has ordered, but also to discover if there is any truth to the rumor that official proceedings are underfoot which, if successful, will take Pearl away from her. "Some of the leading inhabitants" of the colony are of the opinion that Hester is a bad influence on Pearl, or possibly vice-versa; in any event, Governor Bellingham appears to be of their party. Hester brings Pearl along to the Governor's Hall; dressed in livid red, Pearl appears to be "the scarlet letter endowed with life," and so the theme of Pearl's identification with the letter, as its principal effect, is extended. Pearl is therefore both the chief recipient of Hester's love and the emblem of her crime. Some Puritan children take it into their heads to assault Pearl, hurling mud in her direction, but Pearl routs them fiercely; it is not possible to intimidate her.

Hester gains admission to the Governor's somberly luxurious house, filled with ponderous, rich items brought over from England. The walls of the main hall are lined with portraits of Bellingham's ancestors, as grim and cheerless as the family's current representative. Also on display is the Governor's suit of polished armor, throwing off the dazzling rays of the sun. At Pearl's urging, Hester regards her reflection in the breastplate. The curved surface so distorts her appearance that she seems to vanish behind the scarlet letter; clearly, the distorted perspective of the reflection in the Governor's armor is a figure for the exaggeratedly stern and steely point of view of the man himself. Whenever dealing with Puritan subjects, Hawthorne often makes use of their armor as a way of indicating their rigidity and warlike attitude toward the world. So wary are they of injury to their souls that they keep themselves cramped up in heavy and cumbersome emotional and spiritual armor. What's more, their vision of the world is also affected, so that all the bright notes are dulled out, and happiness is disdained or ignored, while all the dark notes, sin and the inevitable judgment of a vengeful God upon the sinner, are emphasized until they alone are visible. Pearl's appearance is altered as well by the armor: she seems to become a leering imp, a monster.

Shaken by what she has seen, Hester leads Pearl to the window, where they may look out over the Governor's garden. Pearl wants one of the Governor's red roses; we are reminded not only of her own red garment and the significance of that color, but also of the rose-bush that grew outside the prison door. At this point, the Governor and the various important persons with whom he has been meeting appear on the garden path.

The scene continues in **"The Elf-Child and the Minister."** Governor Bellingham and John Wilson, both with impressive Old Testament beards, are the first of the procession in the garden. While they are stern Puritans, neither man denies himself a certain legitimate luxury in private, not perhaps entirely commensurate with their public asperity. Arthur Dimmesdale walks behind them, in the company of Roger Chillingworth, who has become his doctor. Dimmesdale's health has been deteriorating, possibly due to overwork, and Chillingworth is treating him; both of them have visibly altered—Dimmesdale is "careworn and emaciated" and as always "pale," while Chillingworth has become "uglier," "duskier," and "more misshapen." The Governor, entering his house, sees Pearl standing alone by the door—Hester being momentarily concealed in shadow. He remarks on Pearl's outlandish attire, and compares her to the "children of the Lord of Misrule." This is a reference to certain English holiday customs, in which the appointed "Lord" is free to parody the vaunting manners of the aristocracy, and the normal social order is playfully turned on its head. Pearl, as a child of the Lord of Misrule, would be a sort of aberration, a figure of mischief. John Wilson, in a spirit of rather dour raillery, asks Pearl if she is "a Christian child" or a fairy. Upon telling them her name, Wilson responds she would be better named for something red, "Ruby, rather!—or Coral!—or Red Rose, at the very least, judging from thy hue!" One must note again that

Pearl is being compared to the roses; like them, she can be both pristine and dangerous.

Upon noting Hester's presence, and whose child Pearl therefore is, the Governor is not so gallant as to refrain from calling Hester "a worthy type of her of Babylon"—a whore, in other words. He accosts her, asking what she could possibly have to teach her child for the salvation of her soul. Hester points to the letter, and says "I can teach my little Pearl what I have learned from this!" The two venerable men decide to test Pearl; Reverend Wilson begins to catechize her, but, although Pearl has been well trained in religious instruction by Hester, she perversely refuses to speak. When they ask her who made her, she insists she was originally a rose, growing on the rose-bush by the prison door. Here again is the willfull conflation, on Pearl's part, of the question of her relationship to her Heavenly Father, the creator of whom the minister and the Governor are speaking, and her relationship to her real, unknown father.

Pearl's apparent ignorance seems to indict Hester as a bad mother, but she, desperate not to lose the only thing left to her in the world, forcefully defends her right to keep Pearl. She even turns to Dimmesdale for help, indirectly and unobtrusively invoking his share in her downfall as reason to intervene on her behalf. Dimmesdale, with his habitual sweetness and eloquence, in a voice which is at once soft and yet so "powerful ... that the hall reëchoed, and the hollow armour rang with it," argues that Hester must be allowed to keep Pearl. God has sent her this child as a blessing and a curse, a lesson to be learned through love, and a means "to keep the mother's soul alive." He means that, had Hester been left with nothing, in bitterness and despair she might have embraced evil ways, or taken her own life (a sin, even among non-Puritans). Dimmesdale makes a convincing case, but his emotional investment in Hester's defense does not go unnoticed by Chillingworth, who is beginning to suspect that Dimmesdale's connection to Hester and Pearl may be more than it appears to be.

As is often the case, Pearl responds to the situation with an uncanny sense of the truth, but without being able to see it or name it for what it is. Dimmesdale's words have somehow reached her elusive heart, and she gently rubs his hand with her cheek in a rare show of human warmth. Ultimately, the Governor and John Wilson decide to leave the matter for the time being, and wait to see how things develop. Hester will keep Pearl for the time being. The chapter, however, is not yet over. As she leaves the Governor's Hall, Hester exchanges words with Mistress Hibbins, who is the Governor's sister, and a witch. She asks Hester if she will come to her witch's sabbath that night, and Hester replies, "I must tarry at home, and keep watch over my little Pearl. Had they taken her from me, I would willingly have gone with thee into the forest, and signed my name in the Black Man's book too, and that with mine own blood!" In other words, Hester is confirming Dimmesdale's suspicion, that without Pearl, she would have abandoned all hope of redemption and even of Christian charity. She would have become a witch: a malefactor, rather than a benefactor, to her community.

With the ninth chapter, "**The Leech**," Hawthorne redirects the reader's attention away from Hester Prynne. Roger Chillingworth is the first real doctor and man of science to practice in Boston, and his medical knowledge is supplemented by a thoroughgoing familiarity with the magical principles of alchemy, and with native lore, acquired during his long captivity. He is associated with supernatural knowledge, a faculty of perceiving hidden and secret things. Perceiving the sudden degeneration of Dimmesdale's health, and perhaps something else—some small clue as to its real cause—he presses his medical services on the minister. Doctors at this time were often referred to as "leeches," since they often employed actual leeches in the treatment of patients; drawing blood was one of the most commonly employed remedies. Chillingworth is a "leech" in both senses of the word: he is a doctor, and he is a parasite. The two men become uncomfortable intimates. Chillingworth attends Dimmesdale nearly at all times, and observes his every action. "He deemed it essential, it would seem, to know the man, before attempting to do him good." But he is doing more than acquainting himself with Dimmesdale's habits and character: he is digging into Dimmesdale, trying to take him apart. There is a veiled aggression in Chillingworth's examinations of Dimmesdale, of which perhaps neither man is fully aware. Chillingworth is, apparently, not fully aware of his own suspicions regarding Dimmesdale; his all-seeing eye proves ironically incapable of turning its gaze back on him.

The two men end up living under the same roof, and, as they cohabitate, Chillingworth's unconscious bitterness becomes increasingly intense, so much so that he is physically altered by it. Rumors begin to circulate to the effect "that the Reverend Arthur Dimmesdale, like many other person of especial sanctity, in all ages of the Christian world, was haunted either by Satan himself, or Satan's emissary, in the guise of old Roger Chillingworth."

Having provided the background information, Hawthorne now moves to a particular scene involving Dimmesdale and Chillingworth in chapter ten, "**The Leech and His Patient**." Having deftly brought the conversation round to the subject of unconfessed sin, Chillingworth inquires of Dimmesdale why a man should refuse to confess his crimes. Dimmesdale responds in the general sense, but indirectly shedding light on the reasons for his own silence: "... guilty as they may be, retaining, nevertheless, a zeal for God's glory and man's welfare, they shrink from displaying themselves black and filthy in the view of men; because, thenceforward, no good can be achieved by them, no evil of the past redeemed by better service." Chillingworth answers that one cannot serve God with "unclean hands," or deny "the shame that rightfully belongs to them."

This conversation transpires by a window in the home Chillingworth and Dimmesdale share; now Pearl and Hester appear in the graveyard outside. Pearl has decorated her mother's letter with burdock burrs, and, seeing Dimmesdale, throws one at him. All the main characters momentarily confront each other, then Pearl leads her mother away through the graves. Something in this moment draws Chillingworth closer to a conscious conclusion about Dimmesdale; he inquires after the minister's health, wondering if perhaps he knows everything there is to know—physical diseases sometimes having spiritual causes. Chillingworth asks Dimmesdale if he will unburden his spiritual troubles to him, and Dimmesdale recoils, refusing. "… not to an earthly physician!" he cries.

Shortly after this minor confrontation, Dimmesdale falls asleep in his chair. Chillingworth enters the room and, in a gentle but terrible moment of trespass, opens Dimmesdale's clothing and peers at his bare chest. Hawthorne has been careful to note several times Dimmesdale's unconscious habit of pressing his hand to his breast when especially troubled, and so it is clear that his illness is related to his chest, the region of his heart. What Chillingworth sees when he looks at Dimmesdale's naked chest is not revealed to us, the readers, but Chillingworth's reaction is: he turns away

> … with what a wild look of wonder, joy, and horror! With what a ghastly rapture, as it were, too mighty to be expressed only by the eye and features, and therefore bursting forth through the whole ugliness of his figure … Had a man seen old Roger Chillingworth, at that moment of his ecstasy, he would have had no need to ask how Satan comports himself, when a precious human soul is lost to heaven, and won into his kingdom.

Because we know Roger Chillingworth has dedicated himself exclusively to the task of discovering the identity of Hester's lover, there is only one plausible interpretation of this scene: something he has seen on Dimmesdale's chest has convinced him, completely and in a single moment, that Dimmesdale is the man he has been seeking.

In **"The Interior of a Heart,"** Hawthorne addresses the question of Chillingworth's subtle motivations. He wants to become as close to Dimmesdale as possible, so as to see as much as he can of Dimmesdale's terrible self-torment; he wants to relish Dimmesdale's suffering as his own revenge. Having discovered the minister's secret, Chillingworth is able to torture him at will—"The victim was for ever on the rack ..."—while maintaining an outward appearance of complete innocence, even benevolence.

And yet, even in the midst of his suffering, "the Reverend Mr. Dimmesdale had achieved a brilliant popularity in his sacred office. He won it, indeed, in great part, by his sorrows." Dimmesdale is a better minister for being a sinner, and a sufferer; his already considerable powers of sympathy are further extended. Unlike his counterparts in the ministry, like John Wilson, he is not an inflexible, judgmental moralist; he is understanding, forgiving, merciful, reverent, respectful. Unfortunately, the warm regard he receives in return for his works only exacerbates his guilt and suffering still further. There have been times when he actually tries to confess from the pulpit, but, in calling himself a sinner, "an abomination," he only impresses the congregation all that much more favorably with his modesty and the severity of his moral self-judgment. Desperate for some means to relieve the intolerable burden of his guilt, he resorts to private, secret self-punishment, lashing his own back with a whip, and denying himself sleep.

"The Minister's Vigil" relates a midnight excursion to the market-square, the scene of Hester's humiliation. This is the first time in the course of the narrative that Hawthorne draws us directly into Dimmesdale's presence, having kept him at a distance until such time as he might reveal, or at least imply, Dimmesdale's share in Hester's downfall. Arriving at the platform on which Hester had stood, Dimmesdale climbs it himself. It being midnight, he will not be seen. He feels as though he bears a scarlet letter over his own heart, where "there had long been, the gnawing and poisonous tooth of bodily pain," and, unable to contain himself, he cries out in anguish. Only two persons respond to his cry—the Governor thrusts his head out his window, holding a lantern, but cannot see Dimmesdale in the dark. And the witch, Mistress Hibbins, likewise peers out of her window and up at the sky, apparently thinking some demon had passed overhead. Both retire again after a few moments.

Then a light appears in the dark; John Wilson himself,

having just attended at the death-bed of Governor Winthrop, is passing, on his way back to his home. Dimmesdale thinks to call out to him, but does not, and Wilson passes without seeing him. Alone again, he imagines himself standing there until the morning light should disclose him to all, and force him to confess. Pearl's mocking laughter breaks upon his reverie; Hester has also been attending on the dying Governor, and is also on her way home in the dark. Dimmesdale calls to them to join him on the platform, and the three of them are united, alone. Pearl asks if he will stand there with them the next day at noon, but Dimmesdale demurs; he claims they will stand together another time, on judgment day. At this moment there is a flash of light in the sky—a meteor, but, to Dimmesdale, it seems as though a gigantic red A appears directly overhead; and, with equal abruptness, Roger Chillingworth is there, watching them. He is the third to come from the Governor's death-bed. Dimmesdale, terrified, asks "Who is that man, Hester?" Hester, keeping her promise, does not answer. In this scene, Hawthorne shows us that there are two sides to Dimmesdale's deception; he is also a victim, in that Chillingworth's power over him depends on his continued concealment of his guilt, and on Hester's refusal to tell who Chillingworth is. Pearl offers to tell Dimmesdale who Chillingworth is, but only babbles nonsense into his ear. "Dost thou mock me now?" he asks her, to which she replies, "Thou wast not bold!—thou wast not true! ... Thou wouldst not promise to take my hand, and mother's hand, to-morrow noontide!" Pearl, as usual, unerringly points to the wrong done to her, and uses it as a pretext to deny love or compassion to others.

In "**Another View of Hester,**" the narrative returns its attention to Hester and Pearl. Meditating on her encounter with Dimmesdale, she is shocked to discover how badly degraded he is in health and mental strength, and resolves to offer him whatever help she can. We learn that roughly seven years have elapsed since the opening of the novel. In this time, strong feelings against Hester have worn away, and the people of Boston have come to regard her in a mixed light. Her charity, goodness, and submission to the judgment against her, have not gone unnoticed; in fact, many regard the A on her breast to mean "Angel," in light of the many good works she has done. While the ministers and colonial authorities continue to employ her as a symbol and an object lesson, "individuals in private life, meanwhile, had quite forgiven Hester Prynne for her frailty." But Hester herself is not unscathed, and has become hard and cold, even repulsive. The years of trial have toughened her, so much so that she is no longer afraid of her husband. Having seen first-hand Dimmesdale's torment, his precarious mental state, and realizing that Chillingworth knows Dimmesdale's secret and is tormenting him, she resolves to remonstrate with her husband.

They speak to each other again, for the second time in the novel, in "**Hester and the Physician.**" Chillingworth now presents a truly demonic appearance; he is hardly human anymore. Hester demands he stop his persecution of Dimmesdale. Contemplating his actions, Chillingworth arrives at a moment of horrified self-knowledge: he realizes he has become a monster. "Not improbably, he had never before viewed himself as he did now." Although he is not mollified, and cannot forgive, he does not oppose Hester when she informs him of her firm intention to reveal his identity to Dimmesdale. They part company.

The following chapter, "**Hester and Pearl,**" opens with a surprising admission of hatred on Hester's part for Chillingworth; she feels his crime in persuading her to marry him is far greater than her crime in betraying that marriage. There follows a rare moment of near-intimacy between mother and daughter; Pearl asks Hester the meaning of the letter, and links it explicitly with the reason Dimmesdale is always pressing his hand to his chest. But Hester cannot answer her daughter's question, and, for the first time, lies about it, claiming she wears it "for the sake of its gold thread." Pearl's momentary warmth toward her mother fades away, but she presses the question, and will not let it go, until Hester is provoked into hostility and threatens to silence Pearl. It is clear that this lasting secret not only stands between Hester and

Pearl, but is poised to grow and thrust them further and further apart.

Chapter sixteen, "**A Forest Walk**," describes how Hester arranges to meet with Dimmesdale by intercepting him on a return trip through the forest. The forest, in *The Scarlet Letter*, is the scene of the putative witches' sabbaths; it is the domain of the native "savages," and the place in which Chillingworth learned some of his medical secrets. Overall, the forest serves Hawthorne as a symbol for a place of license, where the constraints of the city may be thrown off, where sin may take place unpunished, where light and shadow are mixed. Pearl asks Hester to tell her the story of the Black Man, who is the devil as he appears at the sabbath. Mistress Hibbins has told Pearl about him. "Once in my life I met the Black Man" Hester says, "This scarlet letter is his mark!"

Sending Pearl off to play by a babbling brook (to which she bears no small resemblance), Hester withdraws to meet Dimmesdale. They encounter each other in the next chapter, "**The Pastor and His Parishioner**," both of them staring as if the other were a ghost. Dimmesdale complains he has no peace, and can take no solace in the good he does in the ministry; the lie he lives strips everything else of its value. Stricken anew with the deep realization of how much her silence has cost him, Hester can bring herself to reveal her husband's identity only with great effort. Dimmesdale's features darken terribly at the news, but he no longer has the strength even to be angered. "'I might have known it!' murmured he. 'I did know it! ... Why did I not understand?'" Hester embraces him and demands, implores his forgiveness. After a deep and silent inner struggle, Dimmesdale does so, saying "That old man's revenge has been blacker than my sin. He has violated, in cold blood, the sanctity of a human heart. Thou and I, Hester, never did so!"

It gradually becomes clear that Hester and Dimmesdale have come to a crossroads. Dimmesdale cannot bear to remain in Boston, and so Hester tells him he must return to England. Dimmesdale protests he hasn't strength enough to go—not alone. Hester answers, "Thou shalt not go alone!"

In the remarkable chapter that follows, "**A Flood of Sunshine**," the unremitting bleakness of the narrative up to this point gives way to a poignantly brief moment of peace. While no such idea has ever occurred to Dimmesdale, Hester, whose mind is not boxed in by ministerial rules and universal laws, has long been acquainted with the plan in fantasy and speculation. Dimmesdale hardly dares believe it possible; his leaden spirits begin to recover at once. Hester unpins the scarlet letter from her breast and throws it away; she also releases her luxurious and abundant hair from the cap that normally confined it. The life and beauty that seven years of ostracism had ground out of her returns in an instant, and she calls to Pearl, who appears all adorned in flowers and green twigs, like a pagan spirit.

Now Pearl must confront and understand this new turn of events, as described in "**The Child at the Brook-Side**." She is described as "the oneness of their being," the living embodiment of their union. Dimmesdale watches her come with feelings of strong trepidation and anticipation; he wants to love his daughter, and be loved by her, but he understands that, in denying her as his own, he has denied her something precious. Pearl comes up to them on the other side of the brook, and will not cross over, despite Hester's urgings. Frowning, Pearl points rigidly at the spot on her mother's breast where the scarlet letter should be. When Hester becomes angry and orders her to come across to them, which would symbolically represent Pearl's accepting and becoming part of their deceits, Pearl responds by becoming angry herself, and shrieking. She will not even bring her mother the scarlet letter, but insists Hester come over to her side and pick it up. Hester replaces the letter on her bosom, and imprisons her hair under her bonnet again. Only then will Pearl recognize her as her mother; and, when assured that Dimmesdale will not go into town with them, hand in hand, she refuses to have anything to do with him. When he kisses her, she runs back to the brook to wash herself clean of it.

Having utterly destroyed, by the agency of Pearl, any trace of the happiness invoked by their plan, Hawthorne resumes his scrutiny of Dimmesdale in "**The Minister in a Maze**." A "questionable cruiser," bound for Bristol, lies in Boston harbor. Hester, in her charitable work, has become acquainted with the captain of this vessel, and will be able to procure passage for the three of them easily. Even more fortuitously, the ship is not set to depart for another four days: Dimmesdale has been selected to preach the Election Sermon, the most important single function any New England minister could perform, and this sermon is to be delivered in three days. "'At least, they shall say of me,' thought this exemplary man, 'that I leave no public duty unperformed, nor ill performed!'"

In his excitement over the prospect of escape, Dimmesdale begins to unravel mentally. Meeting a venerable deacon in the church, he finds he can barely stop himself from blaspheming in the man's face; meeting an old woman who had lost her entire family, he has difficulty refraining from offering her arguments against the immortality of the soul; he is tempted to join in the indecorous debauches of a group of sailors. Gathering himself together again, he marvels at the near-madness that seems poised to overwhelm him; it seems as though he has made a devil's bargain, to buy happiness at the cost of righteousness, and that the Reverend Dimmesdale who entered the forest is dead and gone, replaced by a new and wholly different man. Returning home, Dimmesdale encounters Chillingworth, and, although they exchange words in their habitual way, Chillingworth discerns at once that Dimmesdale knows his true identity. Dimmesdale dispenses with Chillingworth's medical attention, burns the sermon he had been writing, and sets to work on a new one, which he, in a state of mental exaltation, writes entire in the course of a single night.

Now the pace of the narrative accelerates. In "**The New England Holiday**," we have already reached the day of the sermon. The inhabitants of Boston are preparing for their rather drab festivities. As Hester and Pearl survey the scene, she notes the presence of Roger Chillingworth, deep in conversation with the captain of the Bristol-bound ship. Chillingworth withdraws, and Hester inquires of the captain, privately, what was the matter of his business with the doctor;

he informs her that Chillingworth has booked passage on the same ship, and is resolved to go wherever she and Dimmesdale go. Hester can see Chillingworth smiling blandly at her from across the market-place. She may escape Puritan Boston, but his vengeance will pursue her and Dimmesdale forever, or so he wishes them to think.

In "**The Procession**," the celebration begins in earnest. The various leaders of the Company, civil and religious, parade through the town. Dimmesdale is among their number and, while still physically wasted, he exhibits unusual energy and vigor; he also seems to be caught up in a sort of trance, noticing nothing around him. Mistress Hibbins passes by, laughingly claiming that Dimmesdale, as grand as he might appear, is one of the devil's own; no one seems to take her opinions seriously, however. In the meantime, Dimmesdale has begun to deliver his sermon with all the thrilling and sympathetic power at his command. Hester listens, rapt, but also aware of the unwelcome and judging eyes that continually fall upon her and her letter. Pearl is called a "witch-baby" by one of the sailors, who gives her a message to pass on to Hester, to the effect that Chillingworth will himself place Dimmesdale on the boat, so that Hester need trouble herself about no one but Pearl. A subtle feeling of suspense permeates this chapter, as the novel's events coalesce to the conclusion.

Chapter twenty-three is entitled "**The Revelation of the Scarlet Letter**." The sermon reaches its triumphant end, and Dimmesdale is borne out of the church in a great throng of admiring officials. "He stood, at this moment, on the very proudest eminence of superiority, to which the gifts of intellect, rich lore, prevailing eloquence, and reputation of whitest sanctity, could exalt a clergyman in New England's earliest days...." The procession resumes, but now Dimmesdale appears to have lost all his force; he is so frail he can barely walk, and yet pushes aside all offers of assistance. He approaches Hester and Pearl where they stand, and stops before them, calls them by name. Chillingworth rushes forward with uncanny speed, trying to stop him, but Dimmesdale rebuffs him; it is not clear whether or not he has any knowledge of Chillingworth's plan to accompany them to England. Leaning on Hester, Dimmesdale climbs to the platform on which she was originally exposed, turns to the crowd there assembled, and confesses; he pulls open his clothing and shows his chest to the crowd, to great consternation. Hawthorne is somewhat coy about it, but the reader is plainly meant at least to entertain the idea that the letter A is there, carved into Dimmesdale's flesh. He slumps to the platform nearly fainting, and Chillingworth is at his side, repeating "Thou hast escaped me!" Feeling his life escaping, Dimmesdale asks Pearl if she will kiss him; she does, and

> a spell was broken. The great scene of grief, in which the wild infant bore a part, had developed all her sympathies; and as her tears fell upon her father's cheek, they were the pledge that she would grow up amid human joy and sorrow, nor for ever do battle with the world, but be a woman in it.

It is perhaps only at this point that Hawthorne makes clear the extremity of the stakes involved in Pearl's relationship to her father. Praising God's name, Dimmesdale dies.

In the **"Conclusion,"** we learn that there is considerable disagreement among the public, even among those who were there, as to how Dimmesdale came to have the letter on his chest, or if there were any such letter there at all. Chillingworth, who had lived for years with no other object than revenge on Dimmesdale, falls into a rapid decline and dies less than a year later, leaving Pearl "a very considerable amount of property, both here and in England" in his will. Evidently, Dimmesdale's death may have given him cause to reflect on his malice, and attempt to make amends. Pearl and Hester return to England for a time, but eventually Hester comes back to her modest old home on the outskirts of Boston, still wearing the scarlet letter. Pearl marries into a noble family in England, and Hester is well-provided for in her old age. She continues to do good in the community until her death, and is buried next to Dimmesdale.

The Scarlet Letter is not a love story; none of the characters is able freely to love any of the others. It is not even entirely clear that Hester and Dimmesdale love each other; their "crime" seems to overwhelm and cancel the possibility of any feeling other than shame, excepting those rare moments in which they actually are in each other's presence. They do not pine for each other, and this subtly suggests that their relations have a purely spontaneous and natural character, and therefore that their "crime" is better understood as a momentary lapse in judgment. As for the other characters: an intangible barrier of misfired sympathy separates Hester from Pearl; while Hester wants to give Pearl her love, Pearl refuses to accept it because Hester is withholding her father from her. Chillingworth seems entirely unable to love, his marriage to Hester being a failed attempt to kindle feelings he is no longer able to feel. Love and friendship are alien to the Puritans in general, as Hawthorne depicts them.

Are Hawthorne's Puritans vicious? We understand them to be vulgar, crude, and mob-like. They are unreasoning, unwilling or unable to understand, and without compassion. Do they demand draconian punishment as a compensation for all they have renounced? Do they resent others indulging in those vices they are denied, and avenge themselves? Clearly, the female Puritans resented Hester even before her adultery; she is a "proud beauty," and their unacknowledged jealousy demands her humiliation. The male Puritans do not react to Hester in so general a way; their condemnation has a perfunctory air which in some ways makes it worse. They impose a life-ruining punishment on Hester, and, while they take into account certain mitigating circumstances, they refuse to see her as a person. None of the Puritans of either gender engage with Hester; they deal with circumstances and appearances, not with feelings or motives, and not with spirit.

This is careful on Hawthorne's part: the Puritans are not evil, nor especially cruel; their cruelty, their hypocrisy, their bigotry, are all side-effects of the ubiquitous meanness which is their principal trait. The Puritans depicted by Hawthorne are petty, small-minded, cramped and cramping; they apply a single standard to every element of the great manifold of experiences and events. They are Christian savages, indistinguishable in their essential characteristics from the stereotypical peasants of the Dark Ages—superstitious, dogmatic, provincial in every way. This is part of *The Scarlet Letter*'s sophistication; the Puritans are not merely sinister hypocrites, ready-made villains, like the Catholic Inquisitors of Gothic novels. They are not evil, but they do evil, because they are blind to their own sins. Whenever they encounter something to which they are unable to apply one of their meager handful of formulae, they condemn it out of hand, and then forget all about it. It does not occur to them to question their own practices and motives.

Hawthorne is extremely sensitive to this kind of response to evil; this vehement refusal to examine it, this insistence that it be banished, taken away out of sight at once like a loathsome insect. With considerable psychological acuity, he understands that there may be some deeper reason for this rigid denial, that the rejector may be thereby exhibiting indirectly a sign that he or she has struggled in private with this very evil—that they are perhaps voicing aloud those cries which they normally keep to themselves. But Hawthorne does not restrict his argument to this alone, saying that the Puritans reject Hester only because they secretly hate the moral law that binds them. This will be the case with some, but others condemn her for different reasons; there is a variety of response. Among the Puritans, we see a great deal of automatism, going along with the crowd and/or accepting the rules at face value without inquiring into the reasons for them or the justice with which they are applied and by whom. Christian law has both a letter and a spirit; one must not adhere so strictly to the rules that one loses sight of their original, higher purpose. Any sense of the spirit of the law is badly lacking in the Puritan Boston of *The Scarlet Letter*.

For Hawthorne, one of the greatest possible crimes, and a very common one in any era, is the equation of morality with automatism; that morality is a matter of obeying rules without question. Hawthorne would argue, on the contrary, that moral action is a matter of decision, freely made in the sovereignty of an individual over his own fate. It is the grossest of infractions against another human being to attempt to determine his or her own fate, which is the substance of Hester's punishment. Therefore, *The Scarlet Letter* is not so much the story of a misconstrued crime which is hyperbolically punished by a bigoted community, but a story in which the punishment of a crime is vastly worse than the crime itself Hawthorne only implies, and that not emphatically, that perhaps one might be inclined to see Hester's adultery as something less than a crime. He is deliberately vague about this, not to be coy, but so as not to prescribe to the reader a given moral reading: to do so would be to fly in the face of the novel's whole point, which is precisely that of the freedom of the individual to judge matters morally in accordance with his or her own conscience alone.

Hester, with Hawthorne's tacit approval, utterly defies this prescripted fate and develops her own; for it is not only wrong, but folly, to try to control the fate of another, since we are all, according to Hawthorne, inalienably independent. Chillingworth will learn the same lesson with regard to Dimmesdale. He cannot prevent his public confession: whether or not Dimmesdale remains in Chillingworth's power is entirely up to Dimmesdale. Once he has shaken off Chillingworth's yoke, Dimmesdale cannot be captured again. Dimmesdale escapes strong censure in the unfolding of the novel because he subjects himself to his own grossly exaggerated self-punishment, an effective death sentence. While Hester is an outsider who is publically banished, and while she accepts her guilt and her punishment, she is on one side of this confrontation between the society and the individual—this confrontation which is insisted upon by the community, which needn't have taken place at all were it not for the community's powerful clannish instincts. Dimmesdale, on the other hand, physically embodies this struggle: he is both the sinning individual and representative of the moral (as opposed to the temporal) leader of the community; in a sense, he *is* this community. He is the voice of its moral code, the very code that condemns him. The confrontation between Dimmesdale the sinner and Dimmesdale the minister is played out within his character, and this accounts for his paralysis and his torment. It manifests itself physically in his frenzies and his weariness, and perhaps even in a spontaneous mutilation. As a representative of the whole community, he also seems to embody qualities that imply the presence of barely restrained depravity at times, as during the walk back home from the woods when he can hardly stop himself from acting devilish, shouting insults, carousing with sailors. If he has these impulses, surely the townspeople do, too.

What is the hypocrisy of the Puritans? Certainly not that they all long to do what they condemn in action—this would only be hypocritical if in fact they all were adulterers and Hester were punished only because she was friendless or unlucky. Hawthorne knows better than to make things so easy. So, what is their hypocrisy? It lies in the fact that they profess themselves Christians, and as such are morally obligated to forgive, to accept, to relate to all human beings as human beings first and foremost, as "neighbors," and only thereafter in their particularities, as governor or beggar, man or woman, saint or sinner. But these Christians invert this in practice, they have made Christianity the religion of unflagging judgment, unrelenting punishment, absolute intolerance of any human failing, of even the slightest mistake. And, that being the case, those who have not fallen out of favor must not have made even a single mistake or committed even a single sin, and therefore must be perfect. This is why, in part, Hawthorne is careful to point out that Dimmesdale becomes an even more effective minister as a man with a secret sin on his conscience—this flatly contradicts the idea that the congregation is composed of perfect saints, and it makes a mockery of a society which purports unerringly to search out and punish sin amongst its ranks.

Chillingworth is different; he is not filled with moral outrage at the crime. It is a hideously passionless, cold jealousy that drives him to persecute Dimmesdale, and he perseveres not to satisfy his hatred or injured pride, which would be bad enough, but merely to satisfy his vile curiosity. His vendetta becomes an experiment, at most tinged with hate; the demonic glee that he expresses from time to time is at most only lightly infused with feeling. It is not hate or jealousy that makes him demonic, but this disinterested delight in watching the moral degradation of another human being. The great irony of Chillingworth's character is that, while he in effect has Dimmesdale's soul lying cut open and exposed on a dissecting table, and exhibits expert knowledge of its every feature, his own soul is utterly invisible to him. He does not see or understand with any degree of clarity that his soul is rotting, that he is becoming a monster, that his humanity is dwindling away.

Critical Views

HENRY JAMES ON THE PURITAN MORAL PRESENCE IN HAWTHORNE'S MASTERPIECE

The work has the tone of the circumstances in which it was produced. If Hawthorne was in a sombre mood, and if his future were painfully vague, *The Scarlet Letter* contains little enough of gaiety or of hopefulness. It is densely dark, with a single spot of vivid colour in it; and it will probably long remain the most consistently gloomy of English novels of the first order. But I just now called it the author's masterpiece, and I imagine it will continue to be, for other generations than ours, his most substantial title to fame. The subject had probably lain a long time in his mind, as his subjects were apt to do; so that he appears completely to possess it, to know it and feel it. It is simpler and more complete than his other novels; it achieves more perfectly what it attempts, and it has about it that charm, very hard to express, which we find in an artist's work the first time he has touched his highest mark—a sort of straightness and naturalness of execution, an unconsciousness of his public, and freshness of interest in his theme. It was a great success, and he immediately found himself famous. The writer of these lines, who was a child at the time, remembers dimly the sensation the book produced, and the little shudder with which people alluded to it, as if a peculiar horror were mixed with its attractions. He was too young to read it himself; but its title, upon which he fixed his eyes as the book lay upon the table, had a mysterious charm. He had a vague belief, indeed, that the "letter" in question was one of the documents that come by the post, and it was a source of perpetual wonderment to him that it should be of such an unaccustomed hue. Of course it was difficult to explain to a child the significance of poor Hester Prynne's blood-coloured *A*. But the mystery was at last partly dispelled by his being taken to see a collection of pictures (the annual exhibition of the National Academy), where he encountered a representation of a pale, handsome woman, in a quaint black dress and a white coif, holding between her knees an elfish-looking little girl, fantastically dressed, and crowned with flowers. Embroidered on the woman's breast was a great crimson *A*, over which the child's fingers, as she glanced strangely out of the picture, were maliciously playing. I was told that this was Hester Prynne and little Pearl, and that when I grew older I might read their interesting history. But the picture remained vividly imprinted on my mind; I had been vaguely frightened and made uneasy by it; and when, years afterwards, I first read the novel, I seemed to myself to have read it before, and to be familiar with its two strange heroines. I mention this incident simply as an indication of the degree to which the success of *The Scarlet Letter* had made the book what is called an actuality. Hawthorne himself was very modest about it; he wrote to his publisher, when there was a question of his undertaking another novel, that what had given the history of Hester Prynne its "vogue" was simply the introductory chapter. In fact, the publication of *The Scarlet Letter* was in the United States a literary event of the first importance. The book was the finest piece of imaginative writing yet put forth in the country. There was a consciousness of this in the welcome that was given it—a satisfaction in the idea of America having produced a novel that belonged to literature, and to the forefront of it. Something might at last be sent to Europe as exquisite in quality as anything that had been received, and the best of it was that the thing was absolutely American; it belonged to the soil, to the air; it came out of the very heart of New England.

It is beautiful, admirable, extraordinary; it has in the highest degree that merit which I have spoken of as the mark of Hawthorne's best things—an indefinable purity and lightness of conception, a quality which in a work of art affects one in the same way as the absence of grossness does in a human being. His fancy, as I just now said, had evidently brooded over the subject for a long time; the situation to be represented had disclosed itself to him in all its phases. When I say in all its phases, the sentence demands modification; for it is to be remembered that if Hawthorne laid his hand upon the well-worn theme, upon the familiar combination of the wife, the lover, and the husband, it was, after all, but to one period of the history of these three persons that he attached himself. The situation is the situation after the woman's fault has been committed, and the current of expiation and repentance has set in. In spite of the relation between Hester Prynne and Arthur Dimmesdale, no story of love was surely ever less of a "love-story." To Hawthorne's imagination the fact that these two persons had loved each other too well was of an interest comparatively vulgar; what appealed to him was the idea of their moral situation in the long years that were to follow. The story, indeed, is in a secondary degree that of Hester Prynne; she becomes, really, after the first scene, an accessory figure; it is not upon her the *dénoûment* depends. It is upon her guilty lover that the author projects most frequently the cold, thin rays of his fitfully-moving lantern, which makes here and there a little luminous circle, on the edge of which hovers the livid and sinister figure of the injured and retributive husband. The story goes on, for the most part, between the lover and the husband—the tormented young Puritan minister, who carries the secret of his own lapse from pastoral purity locked up beneath an exterior that commends itself to the reverence of his flock, while he sees the softer partner of his guilt standing in the full glare of exposure and humbling herself to the misery of atonement—between this more wretched and pitiable culprit, to whom dishonour would come as a comfort and the pillory as a relief, and the older, keener, wiser man, who, to obtain satisfaction for the wrong he has suffered, devises the infernally ingenious plan of conjoining himself with his wronger, living with him, living upon him; and while he pretends to minister to his hidden ailment and to sympathise with his pain, revels in his unsuspected knowledge of these things, and stimulates them by malignant arts. The attitude of Roger Chillingworth, and the means he takes to compensate himself—these are the highly original elements in the situation that Hawthorne so ingeniously treats. None of his works are so impregnated with that after-sense of the old Puritan consciousness of life to which allusion has so often been made. If, as M. Montégut says, the qualities of his ancestors *filtered* down through generations into his composition, *The Scarlet Letter* was, as it were, the vessel that gathered up the last of the precious drops. And I say this not because the story happens to be of so-called historical cast, to be told of the early days of Massachusetts, and of people in steeple-crowned hats and sad-coloured garments. The historical colouring is rather weak than otherwise; there is little elaboration of detail, of the modern realism of research; and the author has made no great point of causing his figures to speak the English of their period. Nevertheless, the book is full of the moral presence of the race that invented Hester's penance—diluted and complicated with other things, but still perfectly recognisable. Puritanism, in a word, is there, not only objectively, as Hawthorne tried to place it there, but subjectively as well. Not, I mean, in his judgment of his characters in any harshness of prejudice, or in the obtrusion of a moral lesson; but in the very quality of his own vision, in the tone of the picture, in a certain coldness and exclusiveness of treatment.

The faults of the book are, to my sense, a want of reality and an abuse of the fanciful element—of a certain superficial symbolism. The people strike me not as characters, but as representatives, very picturesquely arranged, of a single state of mind; and the interest of the story lies, not in them, but in the situation, which is insistently kept before us, with little progression, though with a great deal, as I have said, of a certain stable variation; and to which they, out of their reality, contribute little that helps it to live and move. I was made to feel this want of reality, this over-ingenuity, of *The Scarlet Letter*, by chancing not long since upon a novel which was read fifty years ago much more than today, but which is still worth reading—the story of *Adam Blair*, by John Gibson Lockhart. This interesting and powerful little tale has a great deal of analogy with Hawthorne's novel—quite enough, at least, to suggest a comparison between them; and the comparison is a very interesting one to make, for it speedily leads us to larger considerations than simple resemblances and divergences of plot.

Adam Blair, like Arthur Dimmesdale, is a Calvinistic minister who becomes the lover of a married woman, is overwhelmed with remorse at his misdeed, and makes a public confession of it; then expiates it by resigning his pastoral office and becoming a humble tiller of the soil, as his father had been. The two stories are of about the same length, and each is the masterpiece (putting aside, of course, as far as Lockhart is concerned, the *Life of Scott*) of the author. They deal alike with the manners of a rigidly theological society, and even in certain details they correspond. In each of them, between the guilty pair, there is a charming little girl; though I hasten to say that Sarah Blair (who is not the daughter of the heroine, but the legitimate offspring of the hero, a widower) is far from being as brilliant and graceful an apparition as the admirable little Pearl of *The Scarlet Letter*. The main difference between the two tales is the fact that in the American story the husband plays an all-important part, and in the Scottish plays almost none at all. *Adam Blair* is the history of the passion, and *The Scarlet Letter* the history of its sequel; but nevertheless, if one has read the two books at a short interval, it is impossible to avoid confronting them. I confess that a large portion of the interest of *Adam Blair*, to my mind, when once I had perceived that it would repeat in a great measure the situation of *The Scarlet Letter*, lay in noting its difference of tone. It threw into relief the passionless quality of Hawthorne's novel, its element of cold and ingenious fantasy, its elaborate imaginative delicacy. These things do not precisely constitute a weakness in *The Scarlet Letter*; indeed, in a certain way they constitute a great strength; but the absence of a certain something warm and straightforward, a trifle more grossly human and vulgarly natural, which one finds in *Adam Blair*, will always make Hawthorne's tale less touching to a large number of even very intelligent readers, than a love-story told with the robust, synthetic pathos which served Lockhart so well. His novel is not of the first rank (I should call it an excellent second-rate one), but it borrows a charm from the fact that his vigorous, but not strongly imaginative, mind was impregnated with the reality of his subject. He did not always succeed in rendering this reality; the expression is sometimes awkward and poor. But the reader feels that his vision was clear, and his feeling about the matter very strong and rich. Hawthorne's imagination, on the other hand, plays with his theme so incessantly, leads it such a dance through the moon-lighted air of his intellect, that the thing cools off, as it were, hardens and stiffens, and, producing effects much more exquisite, leaves the reader with a sense of having handled a splendid piece of silversmith's work. Lockhart, by means much more vulgar, produces at moments a greater illusion, and satisfies our inevitable desire for something, in the people in whom it is sought to interest us, that shall be the same pitch and the same continuity with ourselves. Above all, it is interesting to see how the same subject appears to two men of a thoroughly different cast of mind and of a different race. Lockhart was struck with the warmth of the subject that offered itself to him, and Hawthorne with its coldness; the one with its glow, its sentimental interest—the other with its shadow, its moral interest. Lockhart's story is as decent, as severely draped, as *The Scarlet Letter*; but the author has a more vivid sense than appears to have imposed itself upon Hawthorne, of some of the incidents of the situation he describes; his tempted man and tempting woman are more actual and personal; his heroine in especial, though not in the least a delicate or a subtle conception, has a sort of credible, visible, palpable property, a vulgar roundness and relief, which are lacking to the dim and chastened image of Hester Prynne. But I am going too far; I am comparing simplicity with subtlety, the usual with the refined. Each man wrote as his turn of mind impelled him, but each expressed something more than himself. Lockhart was a dense, substantial Briton, with a taste for the concrete, and Hawthorne was a thin New Englander, with a miasmatic conscience.

In *The Scarlet Letter* there is a great deal of symbolism; there is, I think, too much. It is overdone at times, and becomes mechanical; it ceases to be impressive, and grazes triviality. The idea of the mystic *A* which the young minister finds imprinted upon his breast and eating into his flesh, in sympathy with the embroidered badge that Hester is condemned to wear, appears to me to be a case in point. This suggestion should, I think, have been just made and dropped; to insist upon it and return to it, is to exaggerate the weak side of the subject. Hawthorne returns to it constantly, plays with it, and seems charmed by it; until at last the reader feels tempted to declare that his enjoyment of it is puerile. In the admirable scene, so superbly conceived and beautifully executed, in which Mr. Dimmesdale, in the stillness of the night, in the middle of the sleeping town, feels impelled to go and stand upon the scaffold where his mistress had formerly enacted her dreadful penance, and then, seeing Hester pass along the street, from watching at a sick-bed, with little Pearl at her side, calls them both to come and stand there beside him—in this masterly episode the effect is almost spoiled by the introduction of one of these superficial conceits. What leads up to it is very fine—so fine that I cannot do better than quote it as a specimen of one of the striking pages of the book.

But before Mr. Dimmesdale had done speaking, a light gleamed far and wide over all the muffled sky. It was doubtless caused by one of those meteors which the night-watcher may so often observe burning out to waste in the vacant regions of the atmosphere. So powerful was its radiance that it thoroughly illuminated the dense medium of cloud betwixt the sky and earth. The great vault brightened, like the dome of an immense lamp. It showed the familiar scene of the street with the distinctness of mid-day, but also with the awfulness that is always imparted to familiar objects by an unaccustomed light. The wooden houses, with their jutting stories and quaint gable-peaks; the doorsteps and thresholds, with the early grass springing up about them; the garden-plots, black with freshly-turned earth; the wheel-track, little worn, and, even in the market-place, margined with green on either side;—all were visible, but with a singularity of aspect that seemed to give another moral interpretation to the things of this world than they had ever borne before.

And there stood the minister, with his hand over his heart; and Hester Prynne, with the embroidered letter glimmering on her bosom; and little Pearl, herself a symbol, and the connecting link between these two. They stood in the noon of that strange and solemn splendour, as if it were the light that is to reveal all secrets, and the daybreak that shall unite all that belong to one another.

That is imaginative, impressive, poetic; but when, almost immediately afterwards, the author goes on to say that "the minister looking upward to the zenith, beheld there the appearance of an immense letter—the letter *A*—marked out in lines of dull red light," we feel that he goes too far, and is in danger of crossing the line that separates the sublime from its intimate neighbour. We are tempted to say that this is not moral tragedy, but physical comedy. In the same way, too much is made of the intimation that Hester's badge had a scorching property, and that if one touched it one would immediately withdraw one's hand. Hawthorne is perpetually looking for images which shall place themselves in picturesque correspondence with the spiritual facts with which he is concerned, and of course the search is of the very essence of poetry. But in such a process discretion is everything, and when the image becomes importunate it is in danger of seeming to stand for nothing more serious than itself. When Hester meets the minister by appointment in the forest, and sits talking with him while little Pearl wanders away and plays by the edge of the brook, the child is represented as at last making her way over to the other side of the woodland stream, and disporting herself there in a manner which makes her mother feel herself, "in some indistinct and tantalising manner, estranged from Pearl; as if the child, in her lonely ramble through the forest, had strayed out of the sphere in which she and her mother dwelt together, and was now vainly seeking to return to it." And Hawthorne devotes a chapter to this idea of the child's having, by putting the brook between Hester and herself, established a kind of spiritual gulf, on the verge of which her little fantastic person innocently mocks at her mother's sense of bereavement. This conception belongs, one would say, quite to the lighter order of a story-teller's devices, and the reader hardly goes with Hawthorne in the large development he gives to it. He hardly goes with him either, I think, in his extreme predilection for a small number of vague ideas which are represented by such terms as "sphere" and "sympathies." Hawthorne makes too liberal a use of these two substantives; it is the solitary defect of his style; and it counts as a defect partly because the words in question are a sort of specialty with certain writers immeasurably inferior to himself.

I had not meant, however, to expatiate upon his defects, which are of the slenderest and most venial kind. *The Scarlet Letter* has the beauty and harmony of all original and complete conceptions, and its weaker spots, whatever they are, are not of its essence; they are mere light flaws and inequalities of surface. One can often return to it; it supports familiarity, and has the inexhaustible charm and mystery of great works of art. It is admirably written.

WILLIAM BYSSHE STEIN ON CHILLINGWORTH'S FAUSTIAN QUALITIES

This technique of interpretation makes the characters most important. Their reactions, to the sin of adultery, the pre-narrative motivation, are the basis of Hawthorne's speculations on the problem of evil and on its associated intellectual and spiritual values. In the case of Chillingworth, who is usually treated as a piece of machinery, a new perspective on his function is afforded, removing the blight of insane jealousy which commonly destroys his real significance. Hawthorne logically motivates all of the physician's actions, and in his plunge to doom there is something of the pathos and tragedy that marked Ethan Brand. Chillingworth, it must be remembered, during most of his life dabbles in magical experiments that fall under the jurisdiction of the devil. Yet, unlike Ethan Brand, he is not impelled by the knowledge which he accumulates to break the magnetic chain of humanity; he continually keeps the welfare of mankind in sight. When he marries Hester, he hopes that she will inspire him to greater efforts. She represents his firmest tie to humanity; she epitomizes its sympathy, tenderness, and love. She links him to the deep heart of the universe. Having a profound faith in the integrity of Hester, he sends her to the New World, intending to follow her after he has arranged his affairs in Europe. Unfortunately, upon arrival he is captured and imprisoned by the Indians. After a lengthy incarceration he is ransomed, and immediately makes his way to the settlement where Hester resides. The first sight that greets his eyes is Hester on the pillory. In the terrible emotional distress that overcomes him, he sees his connection with the magnetic chain of humanity snapped. The grief which floods his heart drives him to a resolution that will, with inexorable finality, exile him from Hester's emotional world. He will, at the propitious moment, sell his soul to the devil, and proclaim his rejection of the brotherhood of man.

To emphasize Chillingworth's essentially heroic stature, Hawthorne sketches him as a Faust, whose prototype we encounter in the dramas. Hester's memories, as she stands on the scaffold, recapture one of her husband's Faustian traits. Her mind's eye dwells on "a pale, thin, scholarlike visage, with eyes dim and bleared by the lamplight that had served them to pore over many ponderous books. Yet those same bleared optics had a strange, penetrating power, when it was their owner's purpose to read the human soul."[5] In the prison-cell scene, as Chillingworth ministers to the ailments of Pearl and Hester, Hawthorne adds another Faustian quality to the scholar's character. Like all Fausts, he has found it necessary to pursue knowledge beyond ordinary limits: and during his captivity with the Indians, he has learned the lore of medicine. Chillingworth, talking to Hester, leaves no doubt about his talents in this study: "My old studies in alchemy ... and my sojourn ... among a people well versed in the kindly properties of simples, have made a better physician of me than many that claim the medical degree."[6] Later Hawthorne imputes the old man's extraordinary skill to magic. An aged craftsman in the village declares that Chillingworth was once an associate of the notorious conjurer, Dr. Froman; and other individuals hint that he "had enlarged his medical attainments by joining in the incantations of the savage priests, who were universally acknowledged to be powerful enchanters, often performing seemingly miraculous cures by their skill in the black art." A vulgar rumor prevails that Chillingworth's dark and ugly face betrays his satanic connections. It is said that "the fire in his laboratory had been brought from the lower regions, and was fed with infernal fuel; and so, as might be expected, his visage was getting sooty with the smoke."[7]

At one point in the narrative Hawthorne makes a direct allusion to the scholar's Faustian antecedents: "... a rumor gained ground, and, however absurd, was entertained by some very sensible people,—that Heaven had wrought an absolute miracle, by transporting an eminent Doctor of Physic, from a German university, bodily through the air, and setting him down at the door of Mr. Dimmesdale's study!"[8] Thus Hawthorne succeeds in endowing Chillingworth with the conventional traits of the familiar Fausts. Scholar, alchemist, magician, and physician, he resembles the Faustian hero who moves across the stage in the first scene of Marlowe's and Goethe's dramas.

Nor does Hawthorne fail to give Chillingworth a glimpse of ideal beauty. The disillusioned scholar confesses that the feelings Hester aroused defied rational definition, as they went beyond the ken of magical explanation: "It was my folly.... I,—a man of thought,—the book-worm of great libraries,—a man already in decay, having given my best years to feed the hungry dream of knowledge,—what had I to do with youth and beauty like thine own!"[9] Yet he concedes that she alone was able to give him a truly human status among his fellow men: "... up to that epoch of my life, I had lived in vain. The world had been so cheerless! My heart was a habitation large enough for many guests, but lonely and chill, and without a household fire. I longed to kindle one! It seemed not so wild a dream ... that the simple bliss, which is scattered far and wide, for all mankind to gather up, might yet be mine."[10] This is the same ghost of beauty that Marlowe's Faustus invoked to ease the shock of disenchantment, the same one also that Goethe's aged Faust deemed a compensation for his failures. In the dream of perfect love they all could identify themselves with mankind.

It is this terrible sense of loss that prompts Chillingworth to bargain away his soul to the devil. He will revenge himself on the criminal who stole Hester's love. And when Hester will not disclose her paramour's name, the old physician grimly asserts: "I shall seek this man, as I have sought truth in books; as I have sought gold in alchemy."[11] In other words, he will read the secret guilt on her betrayer's heart. But the sins that lie hidden in mortal bosoms are not, as Ethan Brand discovered, for the eyes of prying mortals. On Judgment Day they will be disclosed to God who will assign the penalty the sinner must pay! But the Puritan Faust aspires for precisely this knowledge of secret evil. He will render justice in this trespass into the forbidden portals of heaven. He will make a mockery of universal mortality. He will deliberately disown his brotherhood with man and his reverence for God.

In effect, without a formal contract, Chillingworth consummates a pact with Satan. Hawthorne, like Goethe, decrees the volition to evil a sufficient condition of bondage. Yet no doubt is left that the evil controls the will of the scholar magician. After Hester refuses to reveal the identity of her lover, the husband extorts a pledge of silence from her on the legal state of their relations. But something in his cruel smile causes her to regret her promise, and she inquires in fear: "Art thou like the Black Man that haunts the forest round about us? Hast thou enticed me into a bond that will prove the ruin of my soul?" His answer is sardonically elusive: "Not thy soul! No, not thine!"[12] Chillingworth, without as yet being sure of his method, intends to plot against the soul of her unknown lover. The Puritan Faust feels confident that his patience and diabolic art will be rewarded in due time.

In this fashion Chillingworth aligns himself with the demon. He enters into a covenant with the dark evils of his soul. He compromises the integrity of a long life dedicated to the improvement of mankind. Just nine years before, he recalls, his life was "bestowed faithfully for the increase of [his] own knowledge, and faithfully, too, ... for the advancement of human welfare. No life had been more peaceful and innocent than [his]; few lives so rich with benefits conferred."[13] As Hawthorne observes, Chillingworth at first deludes himself that he is the instrument of dispassionate justice. He attempts to rationalize his hate and jealousy as mere intellectual curiosity: "He had begun an investigation, as he imagined; ... desirous only of truth, ... as if the question involved no more than ... a geometrical problem, instead of human passions, and wrongs inflicted on himself." But in a very short time his morbid interest in sin weakens his own resistance to it; his restrained emotions are transformed into a violent impulse of revenge: "... a terrible fascination, a kind of fierce, though still calm, necessity seized the old man within its gripe, and never set him free again until he had done all its bidding."[14] Thus Chillingworth commits spiritual suicide. He has as little control over his moral volition as did the Faust of the chapbook or Marlowe.

At this stage of Chillingworth's development at least three different Faustian variants have influenced Hawthorne's portrayal of the Puritan Faust. First, as in Reynold's *Faust*, he uses the motive of revenge to implement a pact with the devil. Secondly, he skillfully applies Goethe's conception of informal bondage. And thirdly, the corruption of the moral will that informs both the chapbook and Marlowe's Faustus enters into his characterization of his magician. Having at the same time ascribed to the old physician those traits of the Fausts of the dramas and having expertly woven them into the pattern of action, Hawthorne has fabricated a Faust who is indigenous to the New England scene.

Notes

5. *Ibid.*, V, 79–80.

6. *Ibid.*, V, 94.

7. *Ibid.*, V, 156.

8. *Ibid.*, V, 148–149.

9. *Ibid.*, V, 96.

10. *Ibid.*, V, 97.

11. *Ibid.*, V, 98.

12. *Ibid.*, V, 100.

13. *Ibid.*, V, 208.

14. *Ibid.*, V, 158.

HARRY LEVIN ON THE DARKNESS OF HAWTHORNE'S THEME

Having first confronted that book as a classic of the schoolroom, we are cushioned against the shock we should properly feel: the realization that, at the midpoint of the nineteenth century, the primly subversive chronicler of the Puritans could base his first major work on an all but unmentionable subject. Not that this subject, the breach of the Seventh Commandment, is the theme of the book; rather it is the presupposition, the original sin from which everything follows. If there was any pleasure in it, any joy of the senses, that has been buried in the past, and Hawthorne has no intention of reanimating it. But its presence in the accusing shape of the majuscule, insisted on with every appearance of the heroine, lends the most vivid particularity to Hawthorne's general vision of evil, and motivates that unspecified remorse to which his characters are so habitually prone. A is for adultery—could any lesson be plainer than the stigma imposed by his title, "the general symbol at which the preacher and moralist might point?" But morality is not to be so arbitrarily spelled out; nor is it calculated, on this occasion, to warrant any confidence in preachers; and, as for symbols, they derive their ultimate meaning from the emotions with which men and women invest them. The letter A, on the bosom of Chaucer's Prioress, had signified the power of sacred rather than profane love: *Amor vincit omnia*. Hawthorne had even been tempted to ask himself whether another scarlet letter meant "adulteress" or "admirable." By the final phrase of his book, the badge of dishonor has become a heraldic escutcheon: "ON A FIELD, SABLE, THE LETTER A, GULES."

The color-scheme is all the more arresting because the spot of flaming red is set off against the usual background of somber blacks and Puritan grays. The initial sentence introduces a chorus of elders clad in "sad-colored garments," standing before "the black flower of civilized society, a prison." The opening of the prison door is "like a black shadow emerging into sunshine"; but the sunshine, as Hawthorne retrospectively sighed, is conspicuous by its rarity. The dark-haired Hester Prynne, emerging to mount the pillory, babe in arms, is presented as a virtual madonna, despite the token of self-denunciation which she has embroidered into her attire. When the Reverend Mr. Dimmesdale is invited to expostulate with her, "as touching the vileness and blackness of your sin," the irony is precarious; for we are not yet in a position to recognize him as her guilty partner; nor is it until the next chapter that we witness her recognition-scene with her long estranged and elderly husband, who conceals his identity under the name of Chillingworth. The interrelationship between open shame and secret guilt is dramatized by a tense alternation of public tableaux and private interviews. All men are potentially sinners, though they profess themselves saints. Here in old Boston, as in the Salem of "Young Goodman Brown." the Black Man does a thriving traffic in witchcraft. If the letter is his mark, as Hester tells her daughter, it must also be accepted as the universal birthmark of mankind. Once, when she tries to fling it away, it is borne back to her upon a stream; thereafter she accepts it as her doom; she learns to live with it.

Therein she becomes innately superior to those fellow citizens who despise her, and whose trespasses are compounded by their hypocrisies. Their social ostracism may turn her into a "type of ... moral solitude"; but it endows her with "a sympathetic knowledge of the hidden sin in other hearts," which ultimately leads to a kind of redemption, as it does with the virtuous prostitutes of Victor Hugo and Dostoevsky. The letter proves to be a talisman which establishes bonds of sympathy; whereas the proud mantle of Lady Eleanor cut her off from sympathetic involvements. Though Hester lives a life of saintly penance, she does not repent her unhallowed love. On the contrary, she shields her repentant lover, and tells him: "What we did has a consecration of its own." Since their lapse was natural, it is pardonable; it has a validity which her marriage with Chillingworth seems to have lacked. What is unnatural is the pharisaical role into which Dimmesdale is consequently forced. He cannot ease his conscience by wearing a black veil, like the minister of Hawthorne's parable; for he is not mourning the hidden sin of others; he is hiding his own, which is palpable enough. The pulpit and the pillory are the contrasting scenes of his triumph and his self-abasement. His internal anguish, projected against the sky in a gigantic A, is finally relieved when he bares his breast to reveal the counterpart of Hester's letter. Hawthorne is purposefully vague in reporting these phenomena and whether they happen by miracle, hallucination, or expressionistic device. His Dostoevskian point is that every happening must be an accusation to the sinner, who must end by testifying against himself.

Hawthorne rejects an alternative he ironically suggests, whereby the supposedly blameless pastor dies in the arms of the fallen woman in order to typify Christian humility. Nor is her rehabilitation achieved at the expense of the cleric's integrity, as it would be for Anatole France's *Thaïs*. Nor is he thoroughly corrupted, like an evangelical beachcomber out of Somerset Maugham. Arthur Dimmesdale is an unwilling hypocrite, who purges himself by means of open confession. Among the possible morals, the one that Hawthorne selects is: "Be true! Be true! Be true! Show freely to the world, if not your worst, yet some trait whereby the worst may be inferred." Hester is true; and so is Dimmesdale at last; but the third injunction rings hollow. These two have been a sinful pair, and he—by Hawthorne's standard—has been more sinful than she. But the most sinful member of the triangle is, most unnaturally, the injured party. Dimmesdale atones for his trespass by his death; Hester for hers by her life; but for Chillingworth, avenging their violation of his existence, there can be no atonement. "That old man's revenge has been blacker than my sin," exclaims Dimmesdale. "He has violated, in cold blood, the sanctity of a human heart. Thou and I, Hester, never did so." While their trespass has been sensual passion, Chillingworth's is intellectual pride. In short, it is the unpardonable sin of Ethan Brand, of Hawthorne's dehumanized experimentalists, and of that spiritualized Paul Pry whose vantage-point comes so uncomfortably close to the author's. Chillingworth, whose assumed name betrays his frigid nature, plays the role of the secret sharer, prying into his wife's illicit affair, spying upon her lover unawares, and pulling the strings of the psychological romance.

The drama centers less on the colloquies between husband and wife, or those between wife and lover, than on the relationship of lover and husband, each concealing something from the other. "The misshapen scholar" is a man of science, a doctor who treats the agonizing Dimmesdale as his patient. One day the latter inquires where he has gathered such strange dark herbs.

"Even in the graveyard here at hand," answered the physician, continuing his employment. "They are new to me. I found them growing on a grave, which bore no tombstone, nor other memorial of the dead man, save these ugly weeds, that have taken upon themselves to keep him in remembrance. They grew out of his heart, and typify, it may be, some hideous secret that was buried with him, and which he had done better to confess during his lifetime."

"Perchance," said Mr. Dimmesdale, "he earnestly desired it, but could not."

"And wherefore?" rejoined the physician. "Wherefore not; since all powers of nature call so earnestly for the confession of sin, that these black weeds have sprung up out of a buried heart, to make manifest an unspoken crime?"

"That, good sir, is but a fantasy of yours," replied the minister. "There can be, if I forebode aright, no power, short of the Divine mercy, to disclose, whether by uttered words, or by type or emblem, the secrets that may be buried with a human heart. The heart, making itself guilty of such secrets, must perforce hold them, until the day when all hidden things shall be revealed."

If the minister cannot shrive himself, the physician has a disease he cannot cure. Yet it is his concentrated malevolence, more than anything else, that implants the idea of confessing in Dimmesdale's mind. Whether Chillingworth may be his double or else a demon, the spokesman for Dimmesdale's conscience or a devil's emissary—these are possibilities which are raised but scarcely probed. He himself concedes that he is performing a fiend-like office, but considers this "a dark necessity," the inevitable consequence of Hester's downfall, perhaps of Calvinistic predestination. "It is our fate," he warns her. "Let the black flower blossom as it may!" At the outset, when Esther was released from the jail, it was compared to a black flower; and afterward, because Dimmesdale unburdens himself, black weeds will not grow upon his grave. The color of the lovers is red, which stands for blood, for life instead of death; and their expiated sin is incarnate in the elfin fairness of their innocent child, the black-eyed Pearl, whose name betokens purity and whose radiance brings a few sunny touches into the book. When we read, in its concluding pages, that she grew up an heiress and traveled abroad, we realize that we can pursue her further adventures through the novels of Henry James.

The Scarlet Letter, because it is set in the past, is the only romance of Hawthorne's in which the past is not a problem. He contrives a transition to the present, through that convention of the historical novel which evokes the story from faded relics and fictitious documents. The extensive sketch that precedes the extended tale likewise gives him an opportunity, as an evicted job-holder, to make his sardonic farewell to the Custom House. "A better book than I shall ever write was there," he muses as he settles down again in his mirrored chamber, watches the moonlight fusing with the glow of coals at the hearth, and warms to the dream that will convert snow-images into the smouldering creatures of his fiction. Yet, from the midst of his next book, *The House of the Seven Gables*, he pauses to comment: "A romance on the plan of *Gil Blas*, adapted to American society and manners, would cease to be a romance." No, it would be sheer reality; the prospect America spread before the casual traveler, with its crude exertions and its flashy successes, was indeed the stuff of the picaresque novel. Turning home—with a vengeance—to contemporary Salem, Hawthorne was bound to connect it with "a bygone time," and to see that connection as the main issue. Nor could he fail to have been profoundly impressed by the details of a recent local crime—a wealthy householder murdered by his nephew—of which the state's attorney, Daniel Webster, had declared: "Its blackness is not illuminated by a single spark of contrition; not a ray of penitence falls upon it; it is all ink."

DARREL ABEL ON DIMMESDALE AND GOD'S WRATH

How welcome should a *Death in the Lord* be unto them that belong not unto the Devil, but unto the Lord! While we are sojourning in this World, we are in what may upon too many accounts be called *The Devil's Country*: We are where the Devil may come upon us in *great wrath* continually. The day when God shall take us out of this World will be, *The Day when the Lord will deliver us from the hand of all our Enemies, and from the hand of Satan.*

—*The Wonders of the Invisible World*

The fourth and final section of *The Scarlet Letter* shows Dimmesdale, apparently doomed to perdition, spectacularly saved by God's grace. God is the activating agent in this section, and is shown to have been responsible, through his "permissive" power, for the apparently pernicious but actually redemptive actions of Hester and Chillingworth. The minister's dying speech declared that God "hath proved his mercy, most of all, in my afflictions.... Had either [any] of these agonies been wanting, I had been lost forever."

This section (chapters xx–xxiii) is the most artfully handled part of the book. Hawthorne carries forward the impression that evil influences on the minister must be decisive; read anticipatively, the account suggests that Dimmesdale is rapidly declining to perdition. At the same time, the narrative, retrospectively considered, affords evidence that his regeneration was in process. This section is therefore a good example of Hawthorne's famed ambiguity. Although this ambiguity makes explication difficult, it is appropriate for several reasons. It shows that God moves in a mysterious way His wonders to perform. By indicating the turbulence within the minister's mind at this critical time, it renders credible the routing of evil influences by good ones which transpires. By retarding explicit recognition of his regeneration, it effects a dramatic peripety at the end of the story.

The account of Dimmesdale's regeneration faithfully follows orthodox Puritan conceptions, in its specification of the sinner's state before regeneration, of the stages in the actual process of regeneration, and the attitudes invoked toward regeneration.

The sinner was unable to initiate and perfect his own reformation. "It was obvious that men had contrived to bring upon themselves all the anguish they suffered; it was still more obvious that neither this awareness nor the anguish itself liberated them from the trammels of perversity. A being who brought such a destiny upon himself could hardly expect to find within himself the power to master it."[1] "No man can enact regeneration by his own exertion" (Miller, p. 27). God's speech in *Paradise Lost* (II, 173–182) summarizes the orthodox Puritan view:

Man shall not quite be lost, but saved who will;
Yet not of will in him, but grace in me
Freely vouchsafed. Once pure I will renew
His lapsed powers, though forfeit, and enthralled
By sin to foul exorbitant desires:
Upheld by me, yet once more he shall stand
On even ground against his mortal foe—
By me upheld that he may know how frail

His fallen condition is, and to me owe
All his deliverance, and to none but me.

Utter moral incapability is explicitly Dimmesdale's condition at
the beginning of this section. "Deadly sin" was "diffused
throughout his moral system. It had stupefies all blessed
impulses, and awakened into vivid life the whole brotherhood
of bad ones.... [His conduct] did but show his sympathy and
fellowship with wicked mortals, and the world of perverted
spirits."

The last and most ominous sign of the minister's moral
degeneration was the pride with which he looked forward to
his day of worldly exaltation, when he was to preach the
Election Sermon. The conceit of his own piety was the danger
most pernicious to an eminent clergyman: "The Devil
provokes men that are eminent in Holiness unto such things as
may become, eminently *Pernicious*; he provokes them especially
unto *Pride*."[2] "Throughout the seven past years of
Dimmesdale's ministry he had felt agony because in every
pastoral performance "he had spoken the very truth and
transformed it into the veriest falsehood." As he told Hester,
"As concerns the good which I appear to do, ... it must needs be
an illusion." "Puritanism ... demands that the individual
confront existence directly on all sides at once, that no
allowance be made for circumstances or human frailty" (Miller,
p. 45). So long as Dimmesdale's heart acknowledged the truth,
though he could not will his tongue to utter it, he retained an
essential and saving truth in his character: "The only truth that
continued to give Mr. Dimmesdale a real existence on this
earth was the anguish in his inmost soul." But "no man, for any
considerable period, can wear one face to himself, and another
to the multitude, without finally getting bewildered as to which
may be the true." And the minister now calls it "most
fortunate" that his planned elopement with Hester will not take
place until after he enacts what threatens to be his culminating
hypocrisy, the preaching of the Election Sermon. Apparently
the last stage of his "eternal alienation from the Good and
True" was this displacement by pride of his anguished

consciousness of moral truancy; having lost his moral will, he appeared now to have lost the remorse which was its residue and the germ from which it might be revived.

The first event in a sinner's regeneration is "justification." "A change must be wrought in his status before any can be made in his nature" (Miller, p. 27). This change is of course neither conscious nor visible; it is known to have occurred only by the positive regeneration which eventuates. Following the sinner's justification, "divine grace reaches forth to the prostrate man in two ways: first it comes as a call to a new life, a summons from above—which was called 'vocation'" (Miller, p. 27). Hawthorne gives various ambiguous intimations that this call to a new life reached Dimmesdale during the three days between his meeting with Hester in the forest and the preaching of the Election Sermon. The first of these intimations is the composition of the sermon itself, on the night of his return from the forest. Before composing the sermon he still showed signs of the "unaccustomed energy" and "unweariable activity" which had so phenomenally marked the revival of his "strong animal nature." Before composing the sermon, "he ate with ravenous appetite." But "he wrote with such impulsive flow of thought and emotion that be fancied himself inspired." In this passage there are strong evidences of both animal vitality and spiritual influence; the composition of the Election Sermon apparently marks the meeting, interfusion, and transference of powers in Dimmesdale. When Dimmesdale appeared in the procession, on the day of the Election Sermon, everyone remarked that he exhibited more energy than at any time since he "first set foot on the New England shore," and that he no longer held his hand over his heart. Although readers will naturally explain this phenomenal energy as a continuation of the animal vitality aroused by his meeting with Hester, "yet, if the minister were rightly viewed, his strength seemed not of the body. It might be spiritual, and imparted to him angelic administrations." To Hester and Pearl, he seemed not the same man they had so recently conversed with. To Hester, "he seemed remote from her own sphere, and utterly beyond her reach .... She thought of the dim forest ....

How deeply they had known each other then! And, was this the man? She hardly knew him now!" Pearl asked, "Mother, ... was that the same minister that kissed me by the brook? ... I could not be sure it was he; so strange he looked." This passage is the most crucial instance of that ambiguity I have already mentioned. Read anticipatively, with the knowledge given of the minister's moral history, he seems at this point to be a reinvigorated hypocrite; read retrospectively, he is shown to be a man inspired, who has received his "vocation."

The second way in which divine grace "reaches forth to the prostrate man" is by effecting an alteration of the sinner's nature. "It penetrates his being and there it generates—or, in view of Adam's original nature, 're-generates'—a power to respond" (Miller, p. 27). It is this power to respond which Dimmesdale becomes aware of when, passing from the church after the Election Sermon, he meets Hester Prynne at the scaffold and accosts her thus:

> In the name of him, so terrible and so merciful, who gives me grace, at this last moment, to do what—for my own heavy sin and miserable agony—I withheld myself from doing seven years ago, come hither now, and entwine thy strength about me! Thy strength, Hester; but let it be guided by the will which God hath granted me.

Then, "partly supported by Hester Prynne, and holding one hand of little Pearl's," he ascended the scaffold, at midday, in the presence of the multitude, and revealed the scarlet symbol of sin on his "sainted" breast. The sentence in which Hawthorne announces this act of confession is the thrilling climax of the romance: "The sun, but little past its meridian, shone down upon the clergyman, and gave a distinctness to his figure, as he stood out from all the earth, to put in his plea of guilty at the bar of eternal justice."

This "power to respond" which completes the work of regeneration "comes through the impact of a sensible species or phantasm, ... some spoken word or physical experience" (Miller, p. 281). "The means ... may be any experience, ... but ordinarily they are the words of a sermon and the sacraments of the church" (Miller, p. 289). Hawthorne intimates that it was the minister's own sermon that wrought this final operation of grace:

> Never had man spoken in so wise, so high, and so holy a spirit, as he that spake this day; nor had inspiration ever breathed through mortal lips more evidently than it did through his. Its influence could be seen, as it were, descending upon him, and possessing him, and continually lifting him out of the written discourse that lay before him, and filling him with ideas that must have been as marvellous to himself as to his audience.

Thus, at this crisis of utmost peril to his soul, the grace of God filled the faltering minister—an interposition of God which gloriously demonstrated how the mystery of good could overcome the logic of evil. "The moment of regeneration, in which God, out of his compassion, bestows grace upon man and in which man is enabled to reply with belief, was the single goal of the Augustinian piety" (Miller, p. 25). With his last breath, Dimmesdale praised God for thus enabling him "to die this death of triumphant ignominy before the people." ... Compared to this experience of grace, mundane happiness was of little worth. "The burden of Calvinism was that man must find his happiness in the glory and service of God, and not that man may not find happiness. The essence of sin is that man should prefer lesser good ...to 'true virtue.'" "The good which God seeks and accomplishes is the display of infinite being, a good which transcends the good of finite existence."[3]

Some critics, lacking full critical sympathy with Hawthorne and preoccupied with "the good of finite existence," look upon the minister's death as a calamity, and opine that "[if] he had conscientiously been able to flee with [Hester] to a new life on the western frontier, there would have been no tragedy." But this would have been, from Hawthorne's point of view, the greatest tragedy possible for Dimmesdale, for Hawthorne did not identify physical "death and tragedy." Dimmesdale told Hester, "Were I an atheist,—a wretch with coarse and brutal instincts,—I might have found peace, long ere now. Nay, I should never have lost it." To Hawthorne, not physical but moral death was tragic and terrible: "Death is the very friend whom, in his due season, even the happiest mortal should be willing to embrace ... were man to live longer on the earth, the spiritual would die out of him." Death is always in due season when it comes at the right time to keep the spiritual from dying out in man. Even the most sanguine of Transcendentalists, Alcott, wrote, "It is not death but a bad life that destroys the soul." Dimmesdale died in that state of triumphant holiness to which every wayfaring Christian aspires; to him as to Adam "Death becomes / His final remedy" (*Paradise Lost*, XI, 61–62).

Notes

1. Perry Miller, *The New England Mind* (New York, 1939), p. 25.

2. Cotton Mather, *The Wonders of the Invisible World* ("Library of Old Authors," London, 1862), p. 55.

3. Joseph Haroutunian, *Piety Versus Moralism* (New York, 1932), pp. 263, 144.

MARK VAN DOREN ON PEARL

Pearl has for every reader some unreality too, though again the force of the whole tale is natural enough to contain her. She also has something of the supernatural about her; she may even be the devil's child. Something sinister in her, something unpredictable, equals her charm. She is sunshine in her mother's life, and yet her pouts and scowls, her frenzies and her furies, are not the least of Hester's desperations. Her behavior in the forest, when she insists that Hester don again the letter she has cast off, has more meaning than it has at other times. When it is meaningless, as it sometimes is, Hawthorne may be supposed not to have absorbed well enough the notes he made about Una when she was a child of five in Salem.

Hawthorne, watching her then, had been struck by her eccentricity—"a wild grimace, an unnatural tone." She seemed "an unripe apple, that may be perfected to a mellow deliciousness hereafter," but that now was all "acerbity" and discord.

> It seems to me that, like many sensitive people, her sensibility is more readily awakened by fiction than realities.... She is never graceful or beautiful, except when perfectly quiet. Violence—exhibitions of passion—strong expressions of any kind—destroy her beauty.... She plays, sits down on the floor, and complains grievously of warmth. This is the physical manifestation of the evil spirit that struggles for the mastery of her; he is not a spirit at all, but an earthly monster, who lays his grasp on her spinal marrow, her brain, and other parts of her body that lie in closest contiguity to her soul; so that the soul has the discredit of these evil deeds.... There is something that almost frightens me about the child—I know not whether elfish or angelic, but, at all events, supernatural. She steps so boldly into the midst of everything, shrinks from nothing, has such a comprehension of everything, seems at times to have but little delicacy, and anon shows that she possesses the finest essence of it; now so hard, now so tender; now so perfectly unreasonable, soon again so wise. In short, I now and then catch an aspect of her in which I cannot believe her to be my own human child, but a spirit strangely mingled with good and evil, haunting the house where I dwell.

These notes are somehow more convincing than their result in *The Scarlet Letter*. Hawthorne in them is puzzled, not only by what he sees but by the nature of his response—he is not sure he believes any of this, but he says it anyway, and doubtless hopes to forget it. For Pearl, since she exists in public, he has to be more responsible, yet his art does not show him how. Not wholly, that is. Pearl too has her fascinations, and some of them may stem from his very failure to forget the actuality of Una.

At any rate, just as Chillingworth is more interesting than Hawthorne's other villains because we know why he behaves as he does—he is no mere monster of art like Aylmer, Rappaccini, and Ethan Brand—Pearl is Hawthorne's most interesting accident of nature because she is indeed so accidental; and because the fact of her being at all is so painful, so mixed a joy to the more important person, Hester Prynne, by whom she lives.

AUSTIN WARREN
ON DIMMESDALE'S AMBIVALENCE

Hester's conceptions were altered by her experience; Dimmesdale's were not. Unlike her—or (in different and more professional fashion) the nineteenth century agnostics Clough, Arnold, Leslie Stephen, and George Eliot—Dimmesdale was never seriously troubled by doubts concerning the dogmas of Christianity (as he understood them) and the ecclesiastical institution, the church (as he understood it). He was by temperament a "true priest": a man "with the reverential sentiment largely developed." Indeed, "In no state of society would he have been called a man of liberal views; it would always have been essential to his peace to feel the pressure of a faith about him, supporting, while it confined him within its iron framework."

Some aspects of Dimmesdale's rituals would seem to have been suggested by those of Cotton Mather, whom Barrett Wendell, in his discerning study, aptly called the "Puritan Priest." Though Mather's Diary was not published in full till 1911, striking extracts from it appeared as early as 1836 in W. B. C. Peabody's memoir. Dimmesdale's library was "rich with parchment-bound folios of the Fathers and the lore of the Rabbis and monkish erudition ..."; and Mather (possessor of the largest private library in New England) was, as Hawthorne could see from the *Magnalia*, deeply versed in the Fathers and the Rabbis. Those aptitudes were, among the Puritan clergy, singular only in degree. But the "fastings and vigils" of Dimmesdale were, so far as I know, paralleled only by Mather's.

To fasts and vigils, Dimmesdale added flagellations, unneeded by the thrice-married Mather. Dimmesdale's sin, one of passion and not of principle or even of purpose—these three possible categories are Hawthorne's—had been an act committed with horrible pleasurable surprise, after which (since the sin had been of passion) the clergyman had "watched with morbid zeal and minuteness ... each breath of emotion, and his every thought."

It is by his capacity for passion—on the assumption that passionateness is a generic human category, and hence the man capable of one passion is capable of others—that Chillingworth first feels certain that he has detected Hester's lover. Having sketched a psychosomatic theory that bodily diseases may be "but a symptom of some ailment in the spiritual part," the "leech" declares that his patient is, of all men he has known, the one in whom body and spirit are the "closest conjoined," and appeals to the clergyman to lay open any wound or trouble in his soul. Dimmesdale refuses, "passionately," and turns his eyes, "full and bright, and with a kind of fierceness," on the "leech," and then, with a "frantic gesture," rushes out of the room. Chillingworth comments on the betraying passion: "As with one passion, so with another! He hath done a wild thing erenow, this pious Master Dimmesdale, in the hot passion of his heart!"

If a common denominator between a burst of anger and a fit of lust is not immediately apparent, some sharedness there is: in both instances, reason and that persistence we call the self are made temporarily passive. A man's passions are—by contextual definition at least—uncontrollable; they "get the better of" the habitual self. The man "lets himself go"; is "beside himself." It is in this breakdown of habitual control that Chillingworth finds corroboration of what he suspected.

He finds more positive verification when he takes advantage of Dimmesdale's noonday nap to examine his "bosom," there finding, or thinking he finds, the stigma of the scarlet letter branded on the priestly flesh. In view of Hawthorne's emphasis—or, more strictly, Chillingworth's—on the close connection between soul and body in Dimmesdale, this stigma appears to be like (even though in reverse) the stigmata of Christ's wounds which some Catholic mystics have manifested.

Hawthorne turns now to other aspects of Dimmesdale's "case." Consciousness of concealed sin may, like physical deformities, make one feel that everyone is watching him. And inability to give public confession to one's sin, the fact that (through cowardice or whatever) one cannot trust his secret to anyone, may make one equally suspicious of everyone—thus deranging one's proper reliance on some gradated series of trust and confidence.

"Have a real reserve with almost everybody and have a seeming reserve with almost nobody; for it is very disagreeable to seem reserved, and very dangerous not to be so" is the counsel bitter, but not unsage, of Lord Chesterfield. Dimmesdale has a real reserve with everyone and a seeming one, too, save when his passion briefly breaks down his habitual manner. But his cautious guard, his ever vigilant consciousness of what he conceals, has made him incapable of distinguishing between friend and foe, has broken down any confidence in what he might otherwise properly have relied upon, his intuitions. Dimly perceiving that some evil influence is in range of him, and feeling even doubt, fear, sometimes horror and hatred at the sight of the old leech, he yet, knowing no rational reason for such feelings, distrusts the warnings of his deep antipathy.

And now we come to what doubtless most engaged Hawthorne's interest in Dimmesdale: the ambivalence. Dimmesdale's sin and suffering had, in their way, educated the pastor and the preacher. Without his sin of passion and his sin of concealment, Dimmesdale would have been a man learned in books and the abstractions of theology but ignorant of "life," naive, unself-knowing. It was the self-education forced upon him by his sin which made him the pastor, the "confessor," the preacher he is plausibly represented as becoming.

At the end of his seven years, Dimmesdale is a great—or as the American vulgate would have it, "an eminently successful"—pastor and preacher. Hawthorne characterizes the categories into which his fellow-clergymen could be put. Some were greater scholars; some were "of a sturdier texture of mind than his, and endowed with a far greater share of shrewd, hard, iron, or granite understanding" (the preceding epithets show the noun to be used in the Coleridgean, the disparaging, sense); others, really saintly, lacked the Pentecostal gift of speaking "the heart's native language," of expressing "the highest truths through the medium of familiar words and images."

To the last of these categories Dimmesdale might, save for his "crime of anguish," have belonged. This burden kept him "on a level with the lowest," gave him his universal sympathies with the sinful and his sad eloquence, sometimes terrifying, but oftenest persuasive and tender. These sermons made him loved and venerated; but their preacher knew well what made them powerful, and he was confronted with the old dilemma of means and ends.

In the pulpit, Dimmesdale repeatedly intends to make a confession, and repeatedly he does; but it is a "vague," a ritual confession—like that of the General Confession at Anglican Matins, except that "miserable sinner" in whom there is no health is violently intensified by a consistently Calvinist doctrine of total depravity. No difference: Calvinist and Wesleyan and revivalist accusations against the total self can, with equal ease, become ritual. Dimmesdale never specifically confesses to adultery, only to total depravity: "subtle, but remorseful hypocrite," he knows how the congregation will take his rhetorical self-flagellation—as but the greater evidence of his sanctity; for the more saintly a man, the more conscious he is of even the most venial sins.

So the clergyman was fixed in his plight. At home, in his study, he practiced not only his physical act of penance, his self-scourging; but he practiced also a "constant introspection," which tortured without purifying. To what profit this penance unpreceded by penitence, this torturing introspection which led to no resolution, no action?

As he later told Lowell, Hawthorne had thought of having Dimmesdale confess to a Catholic priest (presumably some wandering French Jesuit) as he did, indeed, have Hilda confess to a priest in St. Peter's, not her sin (for she was "sinless") but her complicity by witness to a sin and a crime. Such an idea might have crossed the mind of a Protestant "priest" of Dimmesdale's monkish erudition and practices. But, had he acted upon the impulse, and had the Catholic been willing to hear the confession, there could have been no absolution, either sacramental or moral. Dimmesdale would have had to do real penance, make real restitution, make public confession in unequivocal terms not of his general sinfulness but of his specific sin, the committing of adultery, and of that deeper, more spiritual, sin in which he had persisted for seven years, that of concealing the truth.

What has kept Dimmesdale from confession? Hester has herself been partly at fault, has made a serious error in judgment. At the beginning of the novel, Dimmesdale, her pastor, has, in his public capacity, enjoined her to speak. His injunction that she name her child's father reads ironically as one returns to it after the "seven years" which follow. "Be not silent from any mistaken pity and tenderness for him; for, believe me, Hester, though he were to step down from a high place, and stand there beside thee, on thy pedestal of shame, yet better were it so, than to hide a guilty heart through life. What can the silence do for him, except it tempt him—yea, compel him, as it were—to add hypocrisy to sin? ... Take heed how thou deniest to him—who, perchance, hath not the courage to grasp it for himself—the bitter, but wholesome, cup that is now presented to thy lips!"

Already Dimmesdale had, perhaps, begun to master the art he showed in his later sermons—that of speaking the truth about himself while to others (Hester excluded) he seemed to be uttering a generalization. Arthur Dimmesdale is, "perchance," a coward, weak beside Hester, whose feeling towards him, never contemptuous, partakes certainly of the maternal. Would, she says "that I might endure his agony as well as mine."

If not with all men, with some—perhaps with most, the longer confession is delayed and that, without which confession would scarcely avail—the utmost reparation, restitution, change, conversion, the more difficult it becomes. One "rationalizes" the procrastination—even though the "rationalization" never really satisfies the "rationalizer."

Dimmesdale, as we see him seven years after, appears to offer his basic rationalization in his speech to Chillingworth—expressed (like his injunction to Hester in the third chapter) in generalized, in hypothetical, terms: there are guilty men who, "retaining, nevertheless, a zeal for God's glory and man's welfare, they shrink from displaying themselves black and filthy in the view of men; because, thenceforward, no good can be achieved by them; no evil of the past be redeemed by better services."

There is some truth in what he says. It is a truth known to those who have a jail sentence on their records—or a period of mental illness. And the Catholic Church, which consistently holds that the unworthiness of a priest does not invalidate the sacraments he administers, which conducts its confessions in confessional boxes, not in the presence of a congregation, sees the degree of truth in Dimmesdale's position.

But, for all his Puritan priestliness, Dimmesdale is a Protestant; and the Catholic half-truth—if that is what we should call it—is not for him to appropriate. It is given to Chillingworth to utter the "Protestant" truth. If men of secret sin "seek to glory God, let them not lift heavenward their unclean hands! If they would serve their fellow-men, let them do it by constraining them to penitential self-abasement!"

After her interview with her pastor on the midnight scaffold, Hester is shocked to reflect upon his state. "His nerve seemed absolutely destroyed. His moral force was abased into more than childish weakness." She reflects on her responsibility. Whether Hester's or Hawthorne's—two of her reflections appear to be intended as those of both—the commentator phrasing what Hester feels: "Here was the iron link of mutual crime, which neither he nor she could break. Like all other ties, it brought along with it its obligations." She must disclose to him Chillingworth's identity; must shield her lover.

So Hester assumes her maternal responsibility to her pastor and lover. In "The Pastor and his Parishioner" the roles are ironically reversed. The two meet in the "dim wood," "each a ghost, and awe-stricken at the other ghost." One chill hand touches another almost as chill; yet the grasp of the chill and the chill took away the penultimate chill of isolation which had separated them from all mankind. Their conversation "went onward, not boldly, but step by step...." They "needed something slight and casual to run before and throw open the doors of intercourse, so that their real thoughts might be led across the threshold."

Their first "real thoughts" to find expression are the mutual questions—"Hast thou found peace?" Neither has. Hester tries to reassure Dimmesdale by taking the line, the pragmatic line, which the pastor has already used, in rationalized self-defense, to Chillingworth. He is not comforted. "Of penance I have had enough. Of penitence there has been none!"

Hester sees him, whom she "still so passionately" loves, as on the verge of madness. She addresses him as "Arthur"; throws her arms around him. He is at first violent, with all that "violence of passion" which gave Chillingworth his key. Then he relents: "I freely forgive you now. May God forgive us both!" But he goes on to extenuate his sin by comparison with Chillingworth's: "We are not, Hester, the worst sinners in the world. There is one worse than even the polluted priest! That old man's revenge has been blacker than my sin. He has violated in cold blood the sanctity of a human heart. Thou and I, Hester, never did so!"

Then follow the famous words of Hester. The lovers, like Dante's yet more illustrious couple, had acted in hot blood, not in cold. And—"What we did had a consecration of its own. We felt it so! We said so to each other! Hast thou forgotten it?"

Dimmesdale replies, "Hush, Hester! ... No; I have not forgotten!" That Hester had said so is credible. It is difficult to credit the "priest's" using any such sacred word as "consecration," though Hester remembers the word as used by both; and Dimmesdale—though his "Hush" presumably implies that he in some way now thinks it wrong—does not contradict her recollection.

Now he appeals to Hester to rid him of Chillingworth and what Hester calls the "evil eye": "Think for me, Hester! Thou art strong. Resolve for me! Advise me what to do." And Hester accepts the responsibility. She fixes "her deep eyes" on her lover, "instinctively exercising a magnetic power" over his spirit, now "so shattered and subdued...."

Dismissing Dimmesdale's talk about the Judgment of God, Hester immediately—like a sensible nineteenth century physician or practical nurse—recommends a change of scene, an escape from an oppressive situation, and begins to outline alternate "tours." At first she speaks as though her lover (or former lover—one does not know which to call him) might escape alone: into the Forest to become, like the Apostle Eliot, his recent host, a preacher to the Redmen; or across the sea— to England, Germany, France, or Italy. How, exactly, a Calvinist clergyman, is to earn his living in Catholic France and Italy is not clear; but Hester seems to have unbounded faith in her lover's intellectual abilities and personal power, once he has shrugged off New England: and seems to think of his creed—and even of his profession—as historical accidents. These Calvinists, these "iron men, and their opinions" seem to her emancipated mind to have kept Arthur's "better part in bondage too long already!" He is to change his name, and, once in Europe, become "a scholar and a sage among the wisest and the most renowned of the cultivated world." He is bidden, "Preach! Write! Act! Do anything save to lie down and die!"

In all this appeal, Hester seems projecting her own energy into Dimmesdale and, what is more, seems to show little understanding of her lover's nature: could he, eight years ago, have been a man to whom changing your name, changing your creed, changing your profession could have been thus lightly considered? Can Dimmesdale ever have been a man of action in the more or less opportunist sense of which Hester sees him capable? If so, as an Oxford man (Hawthorne should have made him, as a Puritan, a Cantabrigian), he could have submitted to Archbishop Laud instead of coming to New England. What positive action do we know him to have committed in "cold blood" save that? He committed a sin in hot blood once—it is tempting to say "once," and I often think (unfairly perhaps) that Hester seduced him. Otherwise his sins have been negative and passive—cowardice and its *species*, hypocrisy.

False in its reading of his character and rashly over-sanguine of programs as Hester's exhortation may be, Dimmesdale is temporarily aroused by her strength, by her belief that a man can forget his past, dismiss its "mistakes" and "debts," and start again as though nothing had happened, as though one had neither memory nor conscience. For a moment he believes he can start all over again, if, only, invalid that he is, he had not to start alone. But Hester tells him that he will not go alone: her boldness speaks out "what he vaguely hinted at but dared not speak."

Hester and Arthur part, but not before she had made plans for passage on a vessel about to sail for Bristol. When the priest learns that it will probably be on the fourth day from the present, he remarks, but to himself, not to Hester, on the fortunate timing.

It is "fortunate" because three days hence Dimmesdale is to preach the Election Sermon, the highest civic honor a clergyman could receive. That Dimmesdale should still care, should still look to this ending of his career as a dramatic close, that he should still think of his public duty more than of his private morality shocks Hawthorne as, of all Dimmesdale's doings and not-doings the most "pitiably weak." What is it, finally, but professional vanity? "No man, for any considerable period can wear one face to himself, and another to the multitude, without finally getting bewildered as to which may be the true."

The minister walks home from the Forest "in a maze," confused, amazed. Hester's bold suggestions have temporarily released him from that iron framework which both confines and supports him. His habitual distinctions between right and wrong have broken down; and all that survives is his sense of decorum.

"At every step he was incited to do some strange, wild, wicked thing or other, with a sense that it would be at once involuntary and intentional; in spite of himself, yet growing out of a profounder self than that which opposed the impulse—

"profounder" in a sense Hawthorne does not define. It may be man's subconscious or his "total depravity" left to himself—the Dark Forest in man, the Satanic.

All of his impulses are rebellions against his habitual mode of life and even, one would say, of thought and feeling. Meeting one of his elderly deacons, he has the impulse to utter "certain blasphemous suggestions that rose in his mind respecting the communion supper." And, encountering the oldest woman of his church, pious and deaf and mostly concerned with recollecting her "dear departed," he can think of no comforting text from Scripture but only what then seemed to him an "unanswerable argument against the immortality of the soul," which, happily, she is too deaf to hear. To a pious young girl, he is tempted to give "a wicked look" and say one evil word, and averts the temptation only by rudeness, and to some children, just begun to talk, he wants to teach "some very wicked words." Lastly, meeting a drunken seaman from the ship on which he plans to sail, he longs to give himself with the abandoned wretch—no member of his congregation—the pleasure of "a few improper jests" and a volley of good round oaths; and not his virtue but his "natural good taste" and still more his "habit of clerical decorum" dissuade him.

These temptations exhibit a Dimmesdale I should not have guessed to exist even in unvoiced capacity—and for which Hawthorne has given no preparation: indeed, we are never given any account of the pastor's pre-history at all comparable to that which is furnished for Hester. "The Minister in a Maze" is, indeed, something of a brilliant sketch, a "set piece"— something which occurred to Hawthorne as he was writing his novel, yet not wholly of it. Was the pastor once a young rake that he should know such "wicked words," round oaths, and smutty stories? It is highly unlikely. Intellectual doubts can occur to the most naturally religious of men; and a good man— as well as a man of taste—may hear many words which his principles and his taste would forbid him to use.

Chiefly, I shall have to defend this brilliant chapter on psychological considerations more general than specifically relevant to Hawthorne's protagonist. In the benign phenomenon called "conversion" the selves of a divided self reorder themselves: the self which was dominant is exorcised, or at any event decisively subordinated; the self which existed as subordinate—the "good self"—becomes supreme, or nearly supreme. And there is a corresponding shift of positions which we may call perversion. Both of these changes can, with certain types of men, occur—or show themselves—in a moment. Some of these reorganizations persist; some are brief, impelled as they oftenest appear to be, by the "magnetism" of an emotionally powerful propagandist—such a one as Hester.

In yielding to Hester's proposals of escape, Dimmesdale, says Hawthorne, had, in effect, made such a bargain with Satan as the witch-lady, Mistress Hibbins, suspected him of. "Tempted by a dream of happiness, he has yielded himself with deliberate choice, as he had never done before, to what he knew was deadly sin." This he now has done. Hester, out of one—"humanly speaking"—generous impulse, spared identifying Chillingworth to her lover and *concealed* her lover's name from Chillingworth, and now out of another "generous" impulse she had bade her lover to escape his concealed sin not by now exhibiting himself but by escape from his adopted country, his profession, even his name. And what have been the results of these "generous" impulses—not wholly disinterested, perhaps, since she thinks of being reunited to her lover? What have been the results of these attempts twentieth century Americans understand so well—attempts to help by sparing those we love, or think we love?

Dimmesdale returns to his study, conscious that his old self had gone. The man who returned from the Forest was wiser— wiser about himself, than the man who entered it. But—like Donatello's what a "bitter kind of knowledge." He throws the already written pages of his sermon into the fire, and, after having eaten "ravenously," he writes all night on another.

What, the attentive reader speculates, is the difference between the unfinished sermon written before the Forest and the finished one of the night that followed? That difference, like the nature of the sermon delivered, seems curiously irrelevant to Hawthorne. We are told that the new discourse was written "with such an impulsive flow of thought and emotion" that its writer "fancied himself inspired." Which is the word to be stressed: *fancied* or *inspired*? We are told that he wrote with "earnest haste and ecstasy": where is the stress? Had he something to say in the sermon which was the result of his intention (premeditated at some time before he delivered the sermon) of thereafter taking his stand beside Hester on the Scaffold? Did the sermon have some new tone in it, some tragic or bitter wisdom delivered from that gross lapse into illusion which so bemused and amazed him as he returned from the Forest?

Melville once wrote a masterly and prophetic sermon for Father Mapple. Hawthorne writes none for Dimmesdale. During the delivery of the sermon, we—with Hester—are outside the meeting house. We but hear the preacher's voice, one with great range of pitch, power, and mood. Yet, says Hawthorne, if an auditor listened "intently, and for the purpose," he would always have heard throughout the "cry of pain," the cry of a human heart "telling its secret, whether of guilt or sorrow...." In this respect, however, the present sermon was not unique; for it had always been "this profound and continual undercurrent that gave the clergyman his most appropriate power."

When, after the sermon, we hear dimly from the admiring congregation, its burden, we discover in it—strange to say—that it had ended with a prophetic strain in which, unlike those of the Jewish seers, not denunciation of their country's sins, but foresight of his New England's "high and glorious destiny" had been the theme. I am at a loss to interpret this. That the preacher, about to declare himself an avowed sinner, cannot (like Cotton Mather) denounce his New England's sins, I can see; but why need he celebrate its high destiny? It would appear that Hawthorne, to whom the "subject matter" of the sermon does not seem to matter, has inserted and asserted his own strong regional loyalties!

But I dwell overlong on what, though it ought to matter to the constructor of so closely constructed a novel, seems not to have mattered to Hawthorne. What matters to him, and upon which he is utterly harsh, is that, seeing the error of escape, Dimmesdale has planned first to give the sermon, thus triumphantly ending his professional career, and then to make his public confession. The giving of the sermon as such, and the content of the sermon, don't really concern him—unless the giving of the sermon contributes the publicity and the drama of the Scaffold confession requisite to counterpart the publicity and the drama of that first scaffold on which Hester stood—save for her baby on her arm—alone.

Implied is some final clash of wills and "philosophies" between Hester and Arthur. Dimmesdale bids Pearl and Hester towards the Scaffold. Pearl, bird-like, flies and puts her arms around his knees; but Hester comes slowly, "as if impelled by fate and against her strongest will," and pauses before she reaches him. Only when Chillingworth attempts to stop the pastor's public confession and the pastor again appeals does Hester come. But Dimmesdale has assumed the man's role at last—or *a* man's role: he asks Hester for her physical strength to help him onto the Scaffold, but in asking her strength enjoins, "let it be guided by the will which God hath granted me." When they stand together, he murmurs to Hester, "Is not this better than what we dreamed of in the Forest?" Hester cannot assent. She palliates with "I know not"; then adds what seems to mean "better, perhaps, if we two and little Pearl can die together." But that, though human, is melodramatic. Hester must see that her lover is dying and that there is no way save a supernatural intervention, an "act of God," as insurance companies put it, which can kill her and the child concurrently with him.

After his confession to his parish and the revelation of his *stigma*, he says farewell to Hester. She speaks of their having "ransomed one another" by their consequent miseries, speaks of spending their "immortal life" together. He replies, as he did to her words in the Forest about the private "consecration" of their adulterous union. "Hush, Hester ... The law we broke!— the sin here so awfully revealed—let these alone be in thy thoughts! I fear! I fear!" What he fears is not for his own salvation, assured, to his perception, apparently, by this, his deathbed repentance and confession—but for any reunion of the lovers after death.

TERENCE MARTIN ON HAWTHORNE'S SCAFFOLD SCENES

At the beginning, middle, and end of *The Scarlet Letter* stand Hawthorne's three scaffold scenes. Much emphasis has been placed upon them, and justly so; to know these scenes well is to have a purchase on a romance which is remarkable for its synthesis of elements. Of large structural and thematic significance, each of the scaffold scenes brings together in a moment of moral, emotional, and psychological tension the major characters and forces of the story; concomitantly, each scene centers attention in a dramatic manner on the scarlet letter.

The first scaffold scene, we recall, takes place at midday. For this, as the beadle proclaims, is "the righteous Colony of the Massachusetts, where iniquity is dragged out into the sunshine." As Hawthorne constructs the scene, Hester Prynne stands on the scaffold holding her infant, the people stand below, and the leaders of the community—civil officers, magistrates, ministers—stand above on a balcony. The inhabitants of Boston are thus divided for this scene—the leaders apart and above; and such a division serves Hawthorne's purpose in characterizing both the officials and the people as component parts of this drama.

The officials, clearly, have authority in the matter. Earlier, a group of women outside the jail have muttered about the leniency of Hester Prynne's sentence; in assembly in the marketplace, however, established authority is unchallenged. The leaders of the community—notably Governor Bellingham, the Reverend Mr. Wilson, and the Reverend Mr. Dimmesdale—feel the responsibility of exhorting, commanding Hester to confess the name of her partner. Doubtless, says Hawthorne, these are good men, "just and sage." But out of all humanity, he continues, "it would not have been easy to select the same number of wise and virtuous persons, who should be less capable of sitting in judgment on an erring woman's heart, and disentangling its mesh of good and evil, than the sages of rigid aspect towards whom Hester now turned her face." Indeed, Hester seems convinced "that whatever sympathy she might expect lay in the larger and warmer heart of the multitude."

The idea that sympathy and warmth come from the "people" is, as we have seen, at the very center of Hawthorne's democratic and artistic faith. Committed to a belief in the value of humanity, he would respect the "universal throb" of the human heart and regard the "magnetic chain of humanity" as virtually sacred. But it is the feelings rather than the ideas or perceptions of humanity that are to be trusted. As Hawthorne says in *The Scarlet Letter*: "when an uninstructed multitude attempts to see with its eyes, it is exceedingly apt to be deceived." But when it forms its judgment, "as it usually does, on the intuitions of its great and warm heart, the conclusions thus attained are often so profound and so unerring, as to possess the character of truths supernaturally revealed."

Strong language, this, expressing Hawthorne's fervent commitment to the collective heart of humanity as a fundamental source of wisdom. But, as Hawthorne sees and often say, in his tales of colonial times, this was "not an age of delicacy." The Puritans are stern, somber, and repressive; their children belong "to the most intolerant brood that ever lived." In portraying a Puritan multitude, Hawthorne faces the problem of characterizing sternness and somberness while at the same time remaining true to his faith in humanity. He sports with the Puritans in his description of the Election holiday, saying that they compressed their mirth and public joy into this festal season and thereby so far dispelled their customary gloom that for one day "they appeared scarcely more grave than most other communities at a period of general affliction." Still, despite the lack of popular merriment on this holiday, "the great, honest face of the people smiled, grimly, perhaps, but widely too." Hawthorne sees through Puritan severity to a fundamental humanity; he may castigate or sport with the Puritan posture of grimness, but he cannot repudiate (he can do nothing but admire) the essential humanity that lies under the sad-colored garments of those he is describing. The public is despotic in its temper, he says, incorporating the specific example of the Puritans under this general principle; "it is capable of denying common justice, when too strenuously demanded as a right"; but when, "as despots love to have it," an appeal is made to its generosity, the public frequently awards "more than justice." The seat of generosity is the heart. And in perhaps no other place does Hawthorne repeat so insistently his faith in the great, warm heart of the people as in *The Scarlet Letter*.

The center of attention in the first scaffold scene is, of course, the letter worn by Hester Prynne. "The point which drew all eyes, and, as it were, transfigured the wearer," says Hawthorne, was the "SCARLET LETTER, So fantastically embroidered and illuminated upon her bosom." In this scene the community officially discovers the letter; given the moral imperative that iniquity should be "dragged out into the sunshine," the stares of the townspeople, the "thousand unrelenting eyes ... concentred" on Hester's bosom, constitute a kind of public meditation on the nature of sinfulness and guilt. Toward the end of the scene the Reverend Mr. Wilson, carefully prepared for the occasion, preaches a discourse on sin, "in all its branches, but with continuous reference to the ignominious letter. So forcibly did he dwell upon this symbol," writes Hawthorne, that it assumed new terrors in the people's imagination "and seemed to derive its scarlet hue from the flames of the infernal pit." The letter dominates the scene; it sets Hester apart to such an extent that those who had known her previously "were now impressed as if they beheld her for the first time"; it has the effect of "a spell" which puts her in a "sphere by herself."

As Hester stands on the scaffold, tall, "lady-like," with "dark and abundant hair," the crowd notes with some astonishment that her beauty shines out and makes a halo of her misfortune. From the beginning of her exposure to public view, Hester bears her ordeal with haughty agony. Undeniably she flaunts the letter; yet Hawthorne seems to sympathize with the emotional understanding shown by the youngest matron outside the jail when she says that the pang of the letter will be always in Hester's heart. Alone in the world with the symbol and consequence of her sin, Hester dons an armor of pride that is also a mantle of suffering.

In this initial scene Roger Chillingworth appears on the outskirts of the crowd in a motley civilized and savage costume and soon after experiences an unsettling shock of recognition. Once Chillingworth has recognized Hester on the scaffold, "a writhing horror" twists across his face "like a snake"; for one moment his features are visibly convulsed by a powerful emotion which he quickly controls by an effort of will. Then "the convulsion grew almost imperceptible, and finally subsided into the depths of his nature." When he sees that he is recognized by Hester, "he slowly and calmly raised his finger, made a gesture with it in the air, and laid it on his lips." Chillingworth has repressed his instinctive emotional response to the situation. The snakelike convulsion that expressed his feelings has been pushed deep into his being where it remains as the source of monomania and revenge. And his first message to Hester Prynne is the time-honored gesture of silence and secrecy, the finger raised to the lips. Thus, from the beginning Chillingworth has possessed himself of "the lock and key" of Hester's silence. From the beginning, apparently, he has "resolved not to be pilloried beside her on her pedestal of shame."[3]

On the scaffold with the other leaders of the community stands Arthur Dimmesdale, whose role as Hester's pastor and spiritual mentor forces him to address her and to ask for the name of her partner in sin. In the terrible ambivalence of his position Dimmesdale wants Hester to name him even as he does not want to be named. He would have her pin the letter on him, but he will not reveal his partnership in it. "Be not silent from any mistaken pity and tenderness," he says to Hester; though your partner in sin

> were to step down from a high place, and stand there beside thee, on thy pedestal of shame, yet better were it

so, than to hide a guilty heart through life. What can thy silence do for him, except it tempt him—yea, compel him, as it were—to add hypocrisy to sin? Heaven hath granted thee an open ignominy, that thereby thou mayest work out an open triumph over the evil within thee, and the sorrow without. Take heed how thou deniest to him—who, perchance, hath not the courage to grasp it for himself—the bitter, but wholesome, cup that is now presented to thy lips!

To the multitude, Dimmesdale's appeal seems powerful beyond withstanding. Proof against such emotional eloquence, however, is the man who has it in him to frame the appeal. Even in the first scaffold scene Hawthorne shows forth the deep ambivalence of Dimmesdale's position: the minister would like to be named and known for what he is, an adulterer. Thus, when he speaks the above words to Hester Prynne, the words themselves are true, pathetically so. Being named would bring shame and disgrace, but also the relief of standing clear in one's own identity; moreover, in this community, this "righteous" colony, there is an undeniably correct course of action for Dimmesdale to take—sin and iniquity, he knows, ought to be dragged out into the broad light of noonday. His appeal to Hester is thus pathetically sincere; he is asking her to help him in a way he cannot help himself.

But we gradually come to see why he cannot help himself. For, with all his physical and psychological debility, which makes him seem weak and gives him the posture of a moral invalid deserving of pity (or perhaps contempt), Dimmesdale is afflicted with a devious pride. He cannot surrender an identity which brings him the adulation of his parishioners, the respect and praise of his peers. His contortions in the guise of humility only add to the public admiration which, in turn, feeds an ego fundamentally intent on itself.

After the appeal of Dimmesdale and the harsher stricture of Mr. Wilson have failed to make Hester speak, Chillingworth moves closer to the scaffold and imperiously bids her to name the father of her child. "'I will not speak!' answered Hester, turning pale as death, but responding to this voice, which she too surely recognized. 'And my child must seek a heavenly Father; she shall never know an earthly one!'" After gesturing first for silence, Roger Chillingworth has thus spoken in this first scaffold scene, lending his voice, for personal reasons, to the communal desire for Hester to name her partner. But the gesture of silence has fitted Hester's mood—*The Scarlet Letter* will develop amid the dry regions of silence.

The first scaffold scene concludes (at the end of chapter 3) with a final emphasis on the letter. When Hester is led back to prison, those who peered after her whispered "that the scarlet letter threw a lurid gleam along the dark passage-way of the interior." The Reverend Mr. Wilson has put Hester's letter at the center of his formal discourse; Dimmesdale and Chillingworth have spoken to Hester, overtly and covertly. And the private drama, depending for its form on the silence of the actors, has begun in the midst of communal meditation and a public demand for confession. Thus the terms of the private drama stand opposed to the efforts of the community to have everything immediately out in the open. Those who see the community as a source of all wrong in the romance forget that silence—breeding pride, hypocrisy, and vengeance—is the imposition and the condition of the private drama. But, of course, only in this particular community would silence invoke such subterranean suffering.

Hawthorne's second scaffold scene, which comes precisely at the middle of his romance, turns the moral structure of the first inside out. This is Dimmesdale's scene, staged at midnight rather than at midday. In terms of Puritan orthodoxy it can be nothing but a scene of pseudo-confession, a "mockery of penitence," in Hawthorne's words, a "vain show of expiation." Again Hawthorne emphasizes the letter, this time by stressing Dimmesdale's infatuation with his own guilt. During one of his nights of penance, the thought of going to the scaffold has come over Dimmesdale. Attiring himself with "as much care as if it had been for public worship, and precisely in the same manner," he makes his way to the deserted marketplace. Alone on the scaffold, he feels that the entire world is gazing at the scarlet letter over his heart. His shriek of agony, a good deal more modulated than at first it seems, awakens Governor Bellingham and Mistress Hibbins; but neither sees him on the scaffold. The Reverend Mr. Wilson, returning from the deathbed of Governor Winthrop, walks slowly by the scaffold without noticing Dimmesdale. For darkness is not the medium in which the Puritans recognize sin. Darkness corresponds to secrecy; the midnight scaffold scene is an extension of the private drama. Accordingly, it involves Dimmesdale, Chillingworth, Hester, and Pearl in a unique and lurid confrontation.

Returning homeward with Pearl from the same errand which has brought the Reverend Mr. Wilson and Roger Chillingworth to minister to the final spiritual and bodily needs of Governor Winthrop, Hester is summoned onto the scaffold by Dimmesdale. As he stands with Hester and Pearl, the minister feels the vitality of life other than his own, but he shrinks back from Pearl's request to stand thus together in the broad light of the following noon. The meteor that then lights up the sky bathes them "in the noon of that strange and solemn splendor"; but it is, of course, a false noon, unnatural, lacking moral efficacy.

Hawthorne puts his meteor to good use. It leads him to refer to the New England habit of reading history as God's Providence—of interpreting natural phenomena as signs of special meaning from God to his chosen people. But the massive self-projection of Dimmesdale's guilt also finds embodiment in the meteor. What shall we say, asks Hawthorne, when one man "discovers a revelation, addressed to himself alone," written across the sky: "In such a case, it could only be the symptom of a highly disordered mental state, when a man, rendered morbidly self contemplative by long, interior, and secret pain, had extended his egotism over the whole expanse of nature, until the firmament itself should appear no more than a fitting page for his soul's history and fate." Thus Dimmesdale sees a great scarlet *A* in the sky; cosmic ego evokes cosmic evidence of guilt. But Hawthorne does not dispense with his meteor without a final touch that corroborates Dimmesdale's sense of its shape by illustrating the collective ego of the community. People in the town, Dimmesdale hears the next day, have likewise seen the *A*. "As our good Governor Winthrop was made an angel this past night," the sexton tells him, "it was doubtless held fit that there should be some notice thereof." Hawthorne provides the meteor; history and conscience do the test. And the public and the private worlds in the romance remain apart and opposed.

The same glance that reveals to Dimmesdale the great letter in the sky discloses Chillingworth at the foot of the scaffold. Lighted by the meteor, Chillingworth's features take on a new expression, or, as Hawthorne says, perhaps "the physician was not careful then, as at all other times, to hide the malevolence with which he looked upon his victim." In a setting suggesting to Hester and Dimmesdale the day of judgment, Chillingworth seems "the arch-fiend" himself, come to claim his own. So intense is Dimmesdale's perception of Chillingworth that, when utter blackness succeeds the vivid light of the meteor, the smiling and scowling face of the physician seems somehow to remain, "painted on the darkness," the only reality in an "annihilated" world. "Come good Sir, and my dear friend," says Chillingworth: "let me lead you home." "I will go home with you," replies Dimmesdale. Thus he goes "home" with the man he fears and hates, the man who has discovered the secret of the scarlet letter and whose principle of being has come to depend on its remaining a secret. The nadir of Dimmesdale's moral struggle stands as the moment of triumph for the avenging Chillingworth.

Hawthorne prepares for his third and final scaffold scene by refocusing attention on Hester's scarlet letter. After seven years it has become an object of familiarity in the town. But in the marketplace on Election day are many people from the country who have heard exaggerated rumors about the letter without ever having seen it. They throng about Hester Prynne "with rude and boorish intrusiveness." Noting the curiosity of the crowd, sailors "thrust their sun-burnt and desperado-looking faces into the ring" and Indians fasten "their snake-like black eyes on Hester's bosom." Lastly, their interest in a "wornout subject languidly reviving itself, by sympathy with what they saw others feel," the people of the town torment Hester Prynne, "perhaps more than all the rest, with their cool, well-acquainted gaze at her familiar shame." Thus, just prior to the scaffold scene, "the burning letter ... had strangely become the centre of more remark and excitement, and was thus made to sear her breast more painfully than at any time since the first time she put it on."

The ensuing scene takes its form unexpectedly, amid the wonder of the spectators. Dimmesdale again takes the initiative, this time at midday; he beckons Hester and Pearl to ascend the scaffold with him. Hester's strength is necessary if he is to be "guided by the will which God hath granted" him. At the hour of his greatest public success and triumph ("Never, on New England soil, had stood the man so honored by his mortal brethren as the preacher!"), Arthur Dimmesdale, the spiritual darling of the people, ascends the scaffold with Hester and Pearl. Once again, Roger Chillingworth is present: in the first scaffold scene, he would know the name of Hester's partner; in the second, he does know; and, in the third, he tries desperately to keep others from knowing. Do not perish in dishonor, he whispers in savage fear to Dimmesdale; "I can yet save you." But Dimmesdale repudiates Chillingworth as the tempter, and with the help of God (and Hester) moves toward the freedom of the scaffold. "Hadst thou sought the whole earth over," says Chillingworth, quite in keeping with the dramatic logic of the narrative, "there was no one place so secret,—no high place nor lowly place, where thou couldst have escaped me,—save on this very scaffold!" And Dimmesdale thanks God, assures a doubting Hester that he is doing God's will, and reveals his own scarlet letter to the astonished multitude.

In contrast to the second scaffold scene, which Chillingworth comes to dominate, this final scene remains under the control of Dimmesdale. Perhaps convinced by the towering eloquence of his Election Day sermon, he insists on viewing the world as the creation of a merciful Providence.[4] He cannot agree with Hester when she hopes they may meet in eternity, having "ransomed one another" with all their woe. Only God knows, says Dimmesdale, returning to the subject of his own spiritual drama,

> and He is merciful! He hath proved his mercy, most of all, in my afflictions. By giving me this burning torture to bear upon my breast! By sending yonder dark and terrible old man, to keep the torture always at red-heat! By bringing me hither, to die this death of triumphant ignominy before the people! Had either of these agonies been wanting, I had been lost for ever! Praised be his name! His will be done! Farewell!

The paradox of mercy by affliction thus makes possible the "triumphant ignominy" of Dimmesdale's death. Thankful for the *A*, for Chillingworth, and for the scaffold, the minister has projected an intense religious odyssey, with himself in the heroic central role.[5] His statement that he is "the one sinner in the world" attests to the fusion of guilt and ego that has characterized his life even as it proclaims the omnipotence of the God who can save him. A curious mixture of theology and self, Dimmesdale's ascending faith distances him from Hester and leaves him assured of his own salvation.

Notes

3. Taken out of context, these words (from the beginning of chapter 9) would undoubtedly be seen as a reference to Dimmesdale; that they refer to Chillingworth emphasizes his refusal to acknowledge either Hester or himself and thus points up a subtle analogy between the physician and the minister.

4. For a fuller discussion of the possibility that Dimmesdale may convert himself by means of his own sermon, see my "Dimmesdale's Ultimate Sermon," *Arizona Quarterly* 27 (1971): 230–40.

5. Crews examines this final section of *The Scarlet Letter* carefully in *Sins of the Fathers*, pp. 148–53.

Finally, it is unnecessary to rely on Hawthorne's own sense of parable-making to see how *The Scarlet Letter* dramatically shapes a rhetoric of secrecy. To preserve a sense of Hawthorne's making the novel into a confession is thus to see it, like Dimmesdale's "vague confession," as a "vain show of expiation." We need not suppose that "Hawthorne had been acting the part of each of these characters concealing something of the shame of one and guilt of the other, urgently feigning both a composure and an innocence he knew he had lost"—as Nissenbaum has shown so well.[49] For quite apart from Hawthorne's personal relation to the novel is the text's own means of communicating and intensifying what cannot be said. Not only do the characters connect with each other across these lacunae, but out of the gaps between what the reader apprehends and what cannot be verified emerges the novel's eerily intransigent uncertainty of meanings. The strange, muted violence that bears the novel along—the ravages of the mind, the compromising of the passions, the involutions of the spirit, the dehumanizing power of desire—emerges from the denial of sympathy that underlies nearly every exchange and that animates virtually every conversation. Emerson's famous response to the novel is perhaps more appropriate than at first it might seem: "Ghastly, ghastly," he is reputed to have remarked. That ghastliness is the profound uneasiness into which a reader can fall, the effect of the novel's commitment to balking explicit senses and keeping a secret. As Georg Simmel writes, "the hiding of realities by negative or positive means" is "one of man's greatest achievements.... the secret produces an immense enlargement of life: numerous contents of life cannot even emerge in the presence of full publicity. The secret offers ... the possibility of a second world alongside the manifest world; and the latter is decisively influenced by the former."[50]

An important scene in which this "second world" conditions the "manifest" one occurs when Dimmesdale keeps his vigil while waiting for the Reverend Mr. Wilson's lantern to "reveal his long-hidden secret," so the parson's sin can finally be fully publicized. His "secret" produces an "enlargement of life," or so he allegorically interprets the comet. But in the end, his effort to authenticate this "second world" fails, paralyzed as he is by the "impulse" of "that Remorse which dogged him everywhere" and which drives him "to the verge of disclosure" only to be frustratingly and invariably drawn back into the "tremulous gripe" of "Cowardice." Dimmesdale could neither "endure" nor "fling" his guilt "at once." Instead, "this feeble and most sensitive of spirits could do neither, yet continually did one thing or another, which intertwined, in the same inextricable knot, the agony of heaven-defying guilt and vain repentance" (148). Described here is the duality of keeping a secret, simultaneously wavering between concealment and revelation. For not only does a secret contain "a tension that is dissolved in the moment of its revelation," but also does this moment constitute the "acme in the development of the secret; all of its charms are once more gathered in it and brought to a climax," as seen both in this pivotal episode in the novel (the second of the three scaffold scenes) and in the final revelation. In the earlier scene, the release of a secret's charms is stalled, but in being so, a secret's dual energies redouble, while the pulls acting upon Dimmesdale—Cowardice and Remorse— postpone the climax. The secret is thus "full of the consciousness that it can be betrayed; that one holds the power of surprises, turns of fate, joys, destruction—if only perhaps of self-destruction." The "external danger of being discovered" with which Dimmesdale flirts is "interwoven with the internal danger, which is like the fascination of the abyss, of giving oneself away"—the ever-present potential for a secret's evacuating itself of meaning. For Simmel, "The secret puts a barrier between men, but at the same time, it creates the tempting challenge to break through it, by gossip or confession—and this challenge accompanies its psychology like a constant overtone."[51]

When the anxiety over his imminent betrayal is disappointed, the minister consoles himself with a "grisly sense of the humorous," an overtone to which Hawthorne decidedly gives way in the preface. In Dimmesdale's belief that he need not confess because the coming dawn will reveal his mortification publicly, his "crisis of terrible anxiety" makes an "involuntary effort to disclose itself by a kind of lurid playfulness." Just as he now substitutes himself on the scaffold for Hester and as he will later replace his impenitent self that was lured by his beloved's call for human happiness, Dimmesdale pretends, by fabricating a vision, that he can replace his confession with mediating versions of mortification and debasement. Whether he imagines that the town virgins will expose their breasts to him—inverting his desire—or that he might teach dirty words to children, subvert the spiritual confidence of the old, or trade lewd jokes with sailors, the parson playfully reproduces, as secondarily important, versions of his original sin.[52] These proxies duplicate his sense of his earlier fall to sexual temptation and, as imitations, provide a distorted clue whereby the worst may be inferred. The pleasure that this indirect method affords him is the vicarious one of an originating secret's multiple replications. The "grisly sense of the humorous" can only propel him so far, however; his secret untold, the necessary sympathy not forthcoming, he searches compulsively for more and more precise ways of uncovering his heart to the multitude. Only near the close when confession is imminent does Dimmesdale give the secret voice, in the Election Sermon's resonating "cry of pain," which the reader does not hear. Then can he bare his breast, the final denudation, which the reader is forbidden to see.

Why does the reader not see and hear these most precise versions? Of Hawthorne's belief that he could not, and should not, make a full disclosure but only hint at the worst, thus beseeching the reader's sympathy, Lionel Trilling suggests that the difference between Hawthorne then and now is implied by our impatience with this procedure of masking, hinting, withdrawing. Why not the very worst? Trilling asks. Why keep the secret?[53] For Hawthorne, making the revelation into a riddle is an act of disclosure that elicits the reader's most complete involvement. Rather than divulge the secret of his own experiences or the minister's, Hawthorne attaches this lesson in how to be true "among the many morals which press upon us from the poor minister's experience" (260). It would be "irreverent" to show the worst because it would violate the "sanctity" of the human heart, the sanctity that readers would violate by rending the veil, behind which the author's inmost Me purportedly remains. By the same logic, to show the *A* would be to unmask the worst rather than represent it, however defensively. Exposure would make this moment too much of a lurid sideshow for the multitude Hawthorne was trying to instruct as an audience, especially for the lessons in sympathy he meant to inculcate. Not only would the narrative method of dually promising and postponing a secret's revelation be effectively disrupted, but both the psychological rationale of defense and the moral basis regulating response would also be subverted and undone. Sympathy would no longer be required to apprehend the "black secret in [the] soul" (143).

In *The Scarlet Letter*, Hawthorne devises a system for romance narrative that actively brings the reader into the text. The tactics of representation would seem to suggest that once readers become "kind and apprehensive" they can learn the identity of the novel's "black secret." As the novel develops, however, the very notion of the determinate value of a secret recedes. Instead, the novel's fundamental secret—the meaning of the *A* as one that can be ascribed to Hawthorne—really exists to concentrate the psychological, social, and rhetorical range of several secrets. This concentration of meanings perpetrates a fiction of determinacy through which the reader's sympathy is intensified.

The reader's assurance, then, that one secret needs to be named is a false one. If readers are troubled by Hawthorne's seeming to renege on showing an *A* on Dimmesdale's breast, it is because they are returned to the bewilderment that both preface and romance have promised to relieve. Yet the numerous secrets—of emblem, character, history, and text—would not be accommodated by identifying one secret, for these have been concatenated throughout, from chapter to chapter, scene to scene.

Orchestrating these elements of secrecy, the novel's text, like the *A* itself, offers answers less definitive than organic to the questions it poses. The reader is less a Daniel reading the handwriting on the wall than a member of a community. The text means to shape this society by presenting and reproducing the anxiety of reading, first in the actions of the characters and the interests ascribed, then in the fiction of Hawthorne's reading Surveyor Pue's documents. This anxiety, in Hawthorne's view, will be appeased to the degree that readers are schooled in sympathetic response. When readers are so instructed, they are brought to a knowledge of their own secrets through the leveling process this novel invokes, and a community of readers, like the community of citizens Dimmesdale foresees, can be achieved. This lone note of optimism in Hawthorne's tragic romance must be observed, not merely to be true to the author's characteristic sentimental exertions of hope in the face of evidence he so readily mounts against a society blind to its own lack of sympathy, a society to which the readers of Hawthorne's texts belong. Doomed to live out the logic their secrets demand, the characters collide with or evade each other, embattled as each one is with a "motive secret," caught as they are in conflict with other characters also embroiled in their own secrets. Moreover, this psychological drama is conducted in a community abounding with secrets. Preoccupied with questions of private life and public behavior, this private history of the New England colony suggested, for Hawthorne, still another dimension of secrecy: how the secrets of the past make their presence felt, how the historical present presages the future. In *The House of the Seven Gables*, the secrets of the past and their effect in the present—how the "wrong-doing of one generation lives into the successive ones"— underlie problematic issues of genre and form. The resolutions that Hawthorne finds are to be understood in the ways that the relation between secrets and sympathy illuminates the novel's dynamics of disclosure.[54]

Notes

49. Nissenbaum, 85.

50. Simmel, 330.

51. Simmel, 333–34.

52. I borrow the term *replication* from Brodhead's reading of Pearl's imitative powers, especially as she appears at brook-side. In *Rediscovering Hawthorne* (Princeton: Princeton University Press, 1977), Kenneth Dauber very interestingly observes that *The Scarlet Letter* is "'The Custom-House' writ large" and provocatively suggests that for Hawthorne, "all creation begins in duplication" (97). See "A 'Typical Illusion,'" 87–118.

53. Trilling, 203.

54. On the relation between *The Scarlet Letter* and *The House of the Seven Gables*, see Evan Carton, *The Rhetoric of American Romance: Dialectic and Identity in Emerson, Dickinson, Poe, and Hawthorne* (Baltimore: Johns Hopkins University Press, 1985), 216–18.

CHARLES SWANN ON THE ROLE OF THE CUSTOM HOUSE

It is no longer necessary to argue that "The Custom-House" is to be considered as an intrinsic part of *The Scarlet Letter*—that, in other words, it is a variant on the strategy of *The Story Teller*. It is in "The Custom-House" that Hawthorne offers a semi-fictive genetic account of the origin of his fiction of the scarlet letter, beginning from a reminder of the previous production of his pen ("The Old Manse") before foregrounding the question of the writer/reader relationship. Hawthorne repudiates the romantic ambition "to find out the divided segment of the writer's own nature and complete his circle of existence" but insists that "thoughts are frozen and utterance benumbed, unless the speaker stand in some true relation with his audience" (121). Readers quickly understand the running pun on "custom"—once they realize they have entered the Interpreter's House through which they must pass before encountering the main structure of the story of the letter. The story proper is carefully situated in its social, historical and psychological contexts—for the work of art is not allowed to appear to float free, but is rooted in the concrete historical situation of its genesis and production. It is in "The Custom-House" that Hawthorne launches an investigation of the relationships of fiction to the real world and indicates a subtle and complex inter-relationship between the two worlds. By describing his surroundings in the custom-house he goes a long way towards justifying his historical fiction by suggesting the inadequacies of that way of life. To be a custom-house officer is to be excluded from the ethical world of men in a way which ironically parallels Hester's situation: "the very nature of his business ... is of such a sort that he does not share in the united effort of mankind" (151). Punning on "custom," Hawthorne argues that the experience which is dependent on habit destroys the historical imagination on which a true recognition of reality must be based. The elderly members of the Custom-House are condemned for their inability to have made anything useful or valuable from their pasts. And—given that the stars and stripes flies over the Custom-House, given the explicit references to the patriarchs of the Custom-House— Hawthorne surely intends to suggest a wider placing: is *this* what the seventeenth century patriarchy even with its admitted faults and inadequacies has come to, with its "fortitude ... self-reliance" and "natural authority" (323)?

Seeing Salem as a dust-heap of history, Hawthorne creates the impression that his tale has an authentic base, and obliquely suggests its nature and the nature of his fictional developments, as he famously describes the conditions where his imagination works best: "the floor of our familiar room has become a neutral territory, somewhere between the real world and fairy-land, where the Actual and the Imaginary may meet, and each imbue itself with the nature of the other" (149). But the historical imagination is necessary to perceive the reality of anything but the world of pure objects, as Hawthorne makes clear when discussing the old General. He can be described as he appears, but this is to miss the true, the important realities. The General has a public, an historic identity, but, if that is to be recovered, Hawthorne has to become, so to speak, an archaeologist:

To observe and define his character, however ... was as difficult a task as to trace out and build up anew, in imagination, an old fortress, like Ticonderoga, from a view of its gray and broken ruins. Here and there, perchance, the walls may remain almost complete; but elsewhere may be only a shapeless mound, cumbrous with its very strength, and overgrown, through long years of peace and neglect, with grass and alien weeds. (136)

The General's identity can be recreated, as Hawthorne shows when he looks at him "affectionately." And he suggests that the true reality for the General himself lies within his own consciousness as he recreates and inhabits his past. As the scarlet letter initiates Hawthorne's desire to retell Hester's story and come to terms with old New England, so it is one item from the General's past that makes it possible for Hawthorne to understand him:

There was one thing that much aided me in *renewing and recreating* the stalwart soldier of the Niagara frontier,— the man of true and simple energy. It was the recollection of those memorable words of his,—"I'll try, sir!"—... breathing the soul and spirit of New England hardihood, comprehending all perils, and encountering all. (138–9, my emphasis)

It is the (historical) imagination that makes it possible for Hawthorne to comprehend what the General was—which is at least as important as what he is.

One purpose of "The Custom-House" is, then, to demonstrate that the past can be reconstructed through the sympathetic and informed imagination—an imagination whose other name should be the historical sense. Hawthorne stresses that he has a double past, and with that emphasis he prepares us for his concern with the different but ideally united realms of the public and private sides of human identity which is so crucial in the main story. One of Hawthorne's pasts is his immediate personal past when he defined himself as a writer (but, of course, that is not totally private in that he is also publicly known as a writer—that, after all, is largely why he got the Custom-House job). He emphasizes that the "discovery" of the letter re-awoke his literary feelings and made him realize that neither his own past as writer nor the public, historical past was dead. That fictive fragment from history is presented as having a wider function than re-awakening his old artistic impulses for it also brings into focus a concern with a wider history, with Hawthorne's evocation of the past of Salem and his serio-comic account of his relationship with his ancestors. And, as I began by implying, it is with the way that Hawthorne introduces the letter and the question of its original meaning that it can be seen that, while Hawthorne is profoundly concerned with the functions and powers of symbols, his fiction is really a criticism of symbolic modes of perception and definition—a criticism made in the name of historical, of narrative modes of knowing the world. The fact that the discovery of the only too clearly symbolic A is so obviously at the centre of "The Custom-House" might seem to contradict this. But, as I have tried to suggest, while the reader is told that the letter is an artefact containing considerable power, as long as its meaning remains unknown, which is to say as long as its historical context is unknown, as long as it lacks a placing narrative, it can only communicate itself to Hawthorne's "sensibilities" while "evading the analysis of" his "mind." However "worthy of interpretation" the sign in isolation may be, it cannot be decoded until the accompanying text is read, when it can take its meaning from its place in a story. Until then, what it "signified" is an insoluble "riddle" because of the way in which meanings can be lost from history, "so evanescent are the fashions of the world" (145–6).

Not that Pue's narrative is unproblematic: the discovery of the letter and the text is, of course, a fictional origin for Hawthorne's fiction—an origin that, however, does not significantly contradict the known facts and thus claims the authority of history—or demands, at the least, a willing suspension of disbelief on the part of his audience: "the reader may smile, but must not doubt my word" (146). Yet, however much Hawthorne may claim Pue's story as an authentic authorization for his tale, he almost immediately undercuts that authority in a way that has understandably bothered many readers: "I have allowed ... myself nearly or altogether as much license as if the fact had been entirely of my own invention." Something of a solution to this difficulty lies in the fact that the wearing of an A was a New England punishment for adultery—and in Hawthorne's next paragraph, where he seems to have done his homework in taking an appropriate metaphor from needlework: "There seemed to be here the groundwork of a tale" (147). "Ground-work" is nicely chosen given an OED definition: "The body or foundation on which parts are overlaid, as in embroidery work, painting and the like." The dictionary gives a seventeenth-century (1655) illustration: "In needlework, the sad groundwork is laid before the beautiful colours." The production of the text of *The Scarlet Letter* is, then, presented as analogous to Hester's elaboration of the letter. Hawthorne transforms the sad groundwork of a simple fact about a way that seventeenth-century New England punished adultery into a complex narrative meditation on signs and meanings in history: Hester transfigures a simple sign of society's condemnation of her transgression of its rules into a work of art. And that subversion of the sign of society's intention to define (to limit) the transgressor, to reduce Hester's very self to a sign reading "Thou shalt not ..." problematizes the symbolic definition to which that society is committed and by which the society had intended to limit the transgressor. Society's intention—or, rather, the intention of those in power who claim to represent the society—had been to contain Hester in, so to speak, an eternal present so that her life would largely be constituted by a sense of history as repetition and she would be stripped of the social relationships that make so much of our identity:

> To-morrow would bring its own trial with it; so would the
> next day, and so would the next; each its own trial, and *yet
> the very same* that was now so unutterably grievous to be

borne ... Throughout them all, *giving up her individuality*, she would become *the general symbol* at which the preacher and moralist might point ... Thus the young and pure would be taught to look at her ... as the figure, the body, the reality of sin. (195–6, my emphases)

But that intention to reduce Hester to a government moral health warning would involve the impossible—the elimination of process—whether that process takes the form of the history of a community, of a self, or the interactions between the two.

If the main narrative argues that history will vanquish symbolism's attempt to freeze time and meaning, "The Custom-House" suggests that the present is in any case both a fragile and a problematic concept. There Hawthorne makes a confession of failure yet the very fact of making the confession invites us to consider whether the question of (social) reality in the present is not always dependent on history. His fiction of contemporary life, *The House of the Seven Gables*, is overtly built on history, connecting as the Preface tells us "a by-gone time with the very present that is flitting away from us"—and it is that historical narrative which enables Hawthorne to offer a picture of the modern world (351). One crucial problem in producing or, rather, reproducing the realistic text that Hawthorne might have written instead of *The Scarlet Letter* is the way in which contemporary reality is always vanishing—not so much into history as into limbo because Hawthorne lacks the proper perspective to deal with the experience even though contemporary reality appears to him as an already written text:

A better book than I shall ever write was there; leaf after leaf presenting itself to me, just as it was written out by the reality of the flitting hour, and vanishing as fast as written, only because my brain wanted the insight and my hand the cunning to transcribe it. (151)

Hawthorne fails to write his full-length book about contemporary life partially at least because he could not stop time, because memory is not enough on its own—yet, and surely it is a deliberate irony, one point about "The Custom-House" is that he has shown ways that such a work might be constructed with its necessary roots in private and public history. Another related point is that the difference between Hawthorne's historical romance and a realistic fiction of contemporary life is one of degree, not kind. The rupture with the Custom-House means that the immediate past is in danger of being lost to history even if it is history as autobiography—were it not for "The Custom-House":

> The life of the Custom-House lies like a dream behind me. The old Inspector ... and all those other venerable personages who sat with him at the receipt of custom, are but shadows in my view; white-headed and wrinkled images, which my fancy used to sport with, and has now flung aside for ever. The merchants ...—these men of traffic, who seemed to occupy so important a position in the world,—how little time has it required to disconnect me from them all, not merely in act, but recollection! It is with an effort that I recall the figures and appellations of these few. Soon, likewise, my old native town will loom upon me through the haze of memory, a mist brooding over and around it; as if it were no portion of the real earth, but an overgrown village in cloud-land, with only imaginary inhabitants to people its wooden houses ... Henceforth, it ceases to be a reality of my life.
> (157)

Dream, shadows, images, fancy, haze of memory, mist cloud-land, imaginary: these are the words that Hawthorne uses to describe his sense of his very recent past. This is analogous to the equally radical break with the past evidenced by Hester's reflections in the first scaffold scene where her memories of her European past take the shape of "phantasmagoric forms" under the pressures of the "weight and hardness of the reality" (167). After those phantasmagoric memories have flashed across the screen of Hester's mind, Hawthorne returns to that key term which resonates throughout the novel: reality. The letter, "the infant and the shame were real. Yes!—these were her realities,—all else had vanished!" (168). Hester, having lost her past through her sin and society's punishment of it, has to construct a new history, a new identity for herself which will go beyond the limitations of symbolic definition until, by the end of the novel, there is "a more real life" for her in New England (344). For Hawthorne, all fiction should necessarily be historical fiction—and the worlds both of nineteenth-century Salem and seventeenth-century Boston are not so much to be read as inventions or creations but as re-creations.

Works by Nathaniel Hawthorne

Fanshawe: A Tale, 1828.

Twice-Told Tales, 1837.

Grandfather's Chair: A History for Youth, 1841.

Famous Old People: Being the Second Epoch of Grandfather's Chair, 1841.

Liberty Tree: With the Last Words of Grandfather's Chair, 1841.

Twice-Told Tales, expanded edition, 1842.

Biographical Stories for Children, 1842.

The Celestial Rail-Road, 1843.

Mosses from an Old Manse, 1846.

The Scarlet Letter, 1850.

The House of the Seven Gables, 1851.

A Wonder-Book for Girls and Boys, 1852.

The Snow-Image and Other Twice-Told Tales, 1852.

The Blithedale Romance, 1852.

The Life of Franklin Pierce, 1852.

Tanglewood Tales for Girls and Boys, 1853.

The Marble Faun, published first in England under the title *The Transformation*, 1860.

Our Old Home: A Series of English Sketches, 1863.

Pansie, a Fragment, 1864.

Passages from the American Note-books, edited by Sophia Peabody Hawthorne, 1868.

Passages from the English Note-Books, edited by Sophia Peabody Hawthorne, 1870.

Passages from the French and Italian Note-books, edited by Sophia Peabody Hawthorne, 1871.

Septimus, A Romance, edited by Una Hawthorne and Robert Browning, 1872.

Fanshawe and Other Pieces, 1876.

The Dolliver Romance and Other Pieces, 1876.

Dr. Grimshawe's Secret, A Romance, edited by Julian Hawthorne, 1883.

The Ghost of Doctor Harris, 1900.

Twenty Days with Julian and Little Bunny, 1904.

Annotated Bibliography

Baym, Nina. *The Shape of Hawthorne's Career*. Ithaca, New York: Cornell University Press, 1976.

Byam's book is one of the most widely-read evaluations of Hawthorne's literary development from beginning to end.

Bell, Millicent. *Hawthorne's View of the Artist*. Albany: State University of New York Press, 1962.

This title examines Hawthorne's writing as a reflection of a general theory of art, and his preoccupation with representation.

Crews, Frederick C. *The Sins of the Fathers: Hawthorne's Psychological Themes*. New York: Oxford University Press, 1966.

Crew's book is a psychological/oedipal treatment of selected works. It has long been one of the standard works on Hawthorne.

Dunne, Michael. *Hawthorne's Narrative Strategies*. Jackson, Mississippi: University Press of Mississippi, 1995.

Dunne's book examines how Hawthorne, through the use of various narrative strategies, created text that both enticed yet defied interpretation.

Fiedler, Leslie A. *Love and Death in the American Novel*. New York: Criterion Books, 1960.

Primarily concerned with the American novel's inability to deal with sexuality as well as the novel's obsession with death, Fielder's book includes an influential reading of Hester Prynne as Faust.

Fogle, Richard Harter. *Hawthorne's Fiction: The Light and the Dark*. (Revised edition.) Norman, Oklahoma: University of Oklahoma Press, 1964.

Although the focus is on Hawthorne's shorter fiction, Fogel evaluates Hawthorne's technique in terms of this structural dichotomy; the literary illumination of dark themes and deep and elaborate psychologies. Attention is paid to Hawthorne's use of imagery.

Gerber, John C., editor. *Twentieth Century Interpretations of* The Scarlet Letter. Englewood Cliffs, New Jersey: Prentice-Hall, 1968.

One of the earlier collections of essays concerning *The Scarlet Letter*, Gerber's collection contains many important essays discussing all aspects of the novel, form, and content.

James, Henry. *Hawthorne*. Ithica, New York: Cornell University Press (Reprint edition), 1998.

One of the first in-depth studies of an American author, James's book considers Hawthorne as both a man and a writer. His tender yet critical approach touches upon Hawthorne's preoccupation with evil and guilt.

Matthiesson, F.O. *American Renaissance: Art and Expression in the Age of Emerson and Whitman*. New York: Oxford University Press, 1941.

Mathiesson's book is a crucial study of Hawthorne's place in the efflorescence of American literature in the decades preceding the Civil War. Focused on the five-year period, 1850–1855, Mathiesson concentrates on the authors' conception about nature and literature. Special attention is paid to Hawthorne and *The Scarlet Letter*.

Scharnhorst, Gary (editor). *The Critical Response to Nathaniel Hawthorne's* The Scarlet Letter. Westport, Connecticut: Greenwood Press, 1992.

In this book Scharnhorst collects a thoroughgoing survey of criticism from Hawthorne's contemporaries. Of particular interest are publisher James T. Fields's anecdotal version of the book's composition history, and news accounts of Hawthorne's dismissal from the Salem Custom House.

Stubbs, John C. *The Pursuit of Form: A Study of Hawthorne and the Romance*. Urbana, Illinois: University of Illinois Press, 1970.

This book places Hawthorne's work into the broader context of the romance form, exhibiting Hawthorne's strategies.

Van Doren, Mark. *Nathaniel Hawthorne*. New York: W. Sloane, 1949.

Van Doren's *Nathaniel Hawthorne* remains one of the most literate and well-regarded biographies of Hawthorne.

Waggoner, Hyatt H. *Hawthorne: A Critical Study*. Cambridge, Massachusetts: Harvard University Press, 1955.

Waggoner provides a piece-by-piece dissection of Hawthorne's entire body of work, with special attention to the role of *The Scarlet Letter*.

Contributors

Harold Bloom is Sterling Professor of the Humanities at Yale University and Henry W. and Albert A. Berg Professor of English at the New York University Graduate School. He is the author of over 20 books, including *Shelley's Mythmaking* (1959), *The Visionary Company* (1961), *Blake's Apocalypse* (1963), *Yeats* (1970), *A Map of Misreading* (1975), *Kabbalah and Criticism* (1975), *Agon: Toward a Theory of Revisionism* (1982), *The American Religion* (1992), *The Western Canon* (1994), and *Omens of Millennium: The Gnosis of Angels, Dreams, and Resurrection* (1996). *The Anxiety of Influence* (1973) sets forth Professor Bloom's provocative theory of the literary relationships between the great writers and their predecessors. His most recent books include *Shakespeare: The Invention of the Human* (1998), a 1998 National Book Award finalist, *How to Read and Why* (2000), *Genius: A Mosaic of One Hundred Exemplary Creative Minds* (2002), and *Hamlet: Poem Unlimited* (2003). In 1999, Professor Bloom received the prestigious American Academy of Arts and Letters Gold Medal for Criticism, and in 2002 he received the Catalonia International Prize.

Michael Terry Cisco is a graduate student in the English department of New York University, and author of *The Divinity Student*.

Henry James was a major American-born novelist and critic of the late nineteenth and early twentieth centuries, most widely known for *The Portrait of a Lady* and *The Wings of the Dove*.

William Bysshe Stein was a Professor of English at SUNY Binghamton and author of *Two Brahman Sources of Emerson and Thoreau* and *The Poetry of Melville's Later Years: Time, History, Myth and Religion*.

Harry Levin taught at Cornell University and authored many books, including *Why Literary Criticism Is Not An Exact Science* and *Gates of Horn: A Study of Five French Realists*. He was also one of the principal editors of the *Norton Anthology of English Literature*.

Darrel Abel is author of *The Moral Picturesque: Studies in Nathaniel Hawthorne's Fiction*, and *Ruined Eden of the Present: Hawthorne, Melville, and Poe*.

Pulitzer Prize-winning poet, novelist, and literary critic, **Mark Van Doren** is the author of *Henry David Thoreau* and *The Poetry of John Dryden*.

A fixture at the University of Michigan for twenty years, **Austin Warren** is the author of *In Continuity*.

Widely published and travelled author of *The Instructed Vision: Scottish Common Sense Philosophy and the Origins of American Fiction*, **Terence Martin** has taught in India, Indiana, Dijon, and Poland. His studies of early American writers and pragmatism have appeared in numerous periodicals.

Author of *American Literature, American Culture* and *Immigrant's Voices: Twenty-four Narratives on Becoming an American*, **Gordon Hutner** teaches at the University of Kentucky.

Charles Swann is Reader in the School of American Studies at Keele University, and author of *Nathaniel Hawthorne: Tradition and Revolution*.

Acknowledgments

"Early Years," by Henry James. From *Hawthorne* (Ithaca: Cornell University Press, 1997): 86–95. © 1879 by Henry James. Reprinted by permission.

"*The Scarlet Letter:* The New England Faust," by William Bysshe Stein. From *Hawthorne's Faust: A Study of the Devil Archetype* (Gainesville, FL: University of Florida Press, 1953): 106–110. © 1953 by William Bysshe Stein. Reprinted by permission.

"The Skeleton in the Closet," by Harry Levin. From *The Power of Blackness: Hawthorne, Poe, Melville* (New York: Alfred A. Knopf, 1958): 73–79. © 1958 by Harry Levin. Reprinted by permission of Alfred A. Knopf, a division of Random House, Inc.

"Dimmesdale: Fugitive from Wrath" by Darrel Abel. In *A Scarlet Letter Handbook*, edited by Seymour L. Gross (San Francisco: Wadsworth Publishing Company, 1960): 66–70. ©1960 by Wadsworth Publishing Company, Inc., Belmont, California. All rights reserved. Reprinted by permission.

"*The Scarlet Letter*," by Mark Van Doren. In *Hawthorne: A Collection of Critical Essays*, edited by A.N. Kaul (Englewood Cliffs, NJ: Prentice-Hall, Inc., 1966): 135–136. © 1966 by Prentice-Hall, Inc., Englewood Cliffs, New Jersey. All rights reserved. Reprinted by permission.

"*The Scarlet Letter*: A Literary Exercise in Moral Theology," by Austin Warren. In *The Merrill Studies in* The Scarlet Letter, compiled by Arlin Turner (Columbus, OH: Charles E. Merrill Publishing Company, 1970): 141–151. © 1970 by Charles E. Merrill Publishing Company, Columbus, Ohio. All rights reserved. Reprinted by permission.

Index